5-06

From morning till night, sounds drift from the kitchen, most of them familiar and comforting . . .

On days when warmth is the most important need of the human heart, the kitchen is the place you can find it.

—**E. B. White (1899–1985)**

Authors in the Kitchen

Recipes, Stories,
and More

Sharron L. McElmeel

with Deborah L. McElmeel

LIBRARIES
UNLIMITED
A Member of the Greenwood Publishing Group

Westport, Connecticut • London

Library of Congress Cataloging-in-Publication Data

McElmeel, Sharron L.
   Authors in the kitchen : recipes, stories, and more / by Sharron L. McElmeel with
Deborah L. McElmeel.
    p. cm.
   Includes index.
   ISBN 1-59158-238-5 (pbk.)
   1. Cookery. 2. Children's literature—Authorship. I. McElmeel, Deborah L. II. Title.
TX652.M365 2005
61.5—dc22   2005047484

British Library Cataloguing in Publication Data is available.

Library of Congress Catalog Number: 200547484
ISBN: 1-59158-238-5

First published in 2005

Libraries Unlimited, 88 Post Road West, Westport, CT 06881
A Member of the Greenwood Publishing Group, Inc.
www.lu.com

Printed in the United States of America

The paper used in this book complies with the
Permanent Paper Standard issued by the National
Information Standards Organization (Z39.48–1984).

10 9 8 7 6 5 4 3 2 1

The publisher has done its best to make sure the instructions and/or recipes in this book are
correct. However, users should apply judgment and experience when preparing recipes, especially parents and teachers working with young people. The publisher accepts no respon-
sibility for the outcome of any recipe included in this volume.

Title page photographs: Jane Kurtz (top) kneading dough for orange spirals and Tanya Lee Stone
(bottom) preparing latkes. Photograph of Tanya Lee Stone by Kathy Pentair.

For E. J. M.—and Michael, Deborah
(especially Deborah), Thomas, Steven, Matthew,
Suzanne; and Michael, Jade, Aubrey, E. J.,
Kylie, and Kaydence.

Contents

Introduction ix

David A. Adler—Birthday Cake 1
Laurie Halse Anderson—Cranberry Jell-O 5
Caroline Arnold—Anasazi Bean Soup 9
Jim Aylesworth—Fudge 13
Mary Azarian—Cinnamon Rolls 17
Bob Barner—Pecan Pie 21
Raymond Bial—German Potato Salad 25
Ashley Bryan—Sweet Potato Pie 29
Eve Bunting—Birthday Cake 33
Dori Hillestad Butler—Lefse 37
Toni Buzzeo—Pumpkin Pie Pizzazz 41
Janie Bynum—Banana Bread 45
Eric Carle—German Style Potato Dumplings 49
Mary Casanova—Crazy Chocolate Cake 53
Judith Caseley—Broccoli, Cookies, and More 57
Shirley Climo—Sherbet 61
Susan Stevens Crummel—Mexican Roll-ups 65
Pat Cummings—Chocolate Chip Cookies 69
Carl Deuker—Vegetable Medley 73
Diane Dillon and Leo Dillon—Plantain Fritters 77
Marianne J. Dyson—Saffron Chicken 81
Kathy Feeney—Marco Polo Bars 85
Debra Frasier—Orange Ambrosia 89
Susan Gaber—Cucumbers 93
Gail Gibbons—Apple Pie 97
Paul Goble—Buffalo Berry Preserves 101
Carol Gorman—Spaghetti 105
Dan Gutman—Fruit 109
Esther Hershenhorn—Chicken Soup 113
Trina Schart Hyman and Katrin Tchana—Sweet Rice Cakes 117
Paul Brett Johnson—Fried Chicken 121
Keiko Kasza—Potato Salad 125
Steven Kellogg—Hot Marshmallow Cheesecake with Raspberry Fudge Sauce 129
Jane Kurtz—Orange Spirals 133
Elaine Landau—Scalloped Corn 137
Deborah Nourse Lattimore—Shrimp Santorini 141
Melinda Long—Bumblebee Stew 145
Betsy Maestro—Sour Cream Cookies 149

Jacqueline Briggs Martin—Coconut Cake 153
Yuyi Morales—Tortillas 157
Nancy Winslow Parker—Pound Cake 161
John Paterson and Katherine Paterson—Blueberry Muffins 165
Jeni Reeves—Chess Pie 169
Dian Curtis Regan—Brownies 173
Barbara Santucci—Zucchini Bread 177
April Pulley Sayre—Pasta 181
Janet Stevens—Vegetable Soup 185
Tanya Lee Stone—Latkes 189
Anastasia Suen—Chocolate Chip Cookies 193
Jane Yolen and Heidi Elizabet Yolen Stemple—Chocolate. 197

Photograph Credits 201
Illustrative Credits 202
Quotation Credits 203
Acknowledgments of Recipe Sources 205
Sources for More Information 206

Indices
General—Theme/Subject 207
Recipe 213

Introduction

This book is simply a book for lovers of food and books. We—Deborah and I, are both. Deborah grew up in our family household filled with books. Although I make a great pumpkin pie and a few other specialties, I am not a great cook, but Deborah surely is. She knows a good recipe when she sees one, and we both know books and authors.

For this cookbook we have solicited stories and recipes from many of our favorite authors and illustrators. Some of the recipes are family recipes generously sent by an author. Those recipes are designated "signature recipes" and are "signed" by the author. Other recipes have been developed especially to connect with an author's story from his or her life or a book he or she has written. To complement those recipes we have added stories and bits and pieces of information that will help readers make literary connections to the food. We hope some connections will spur interest in learning more about a topic or subject.

Our thanks to each of the fifty-four authors and illustrators represented here. Some sent recipes, others sent stories, and some sent both. Each sent correspondence that allowed us to connect an idea with them or their book.

In addition, we'd like to add a thank you to other individuals who contributed their own or family recipes. Elaine Martindale, Ashley Bryan's sister, was kind enough to send her comments and recipes along to complement the information sent by her brother. Katherine Hanson, an avid teen-age reader, sent along her recipe for hot chocolate to correspond with the entry for Jane Yolen and Heidi Elisabet Yolen Stemple. Thanks to Yana Cutler, the current co-proprietor of the Ronneburg Restaurant in Amana, Iowa, we were able to contact Elsie Oehler, the legendary cook from the Ronneburg Restaurant in Amana and the author of *Ronneburg Recipe Album* who generously allowed us to reprint her authentic German recipes for Eric Carle's section in this book.

Mary Azarian, Janie Bynum, Paul Goble, Trina Schart Hyman, Steven Kellogg, Nancy Winslow Parker, and Jeni Reeves each sent along illustrations for their section—a special addition to their comments and stories. The illustration by Hyman was sent shortly before she succumbed to cancer in November 2004. Others such as Jane Kurtz, Tanya Lee Stone, Heidi E. Y. Stemple, Jane Yolen, Sandy Lanton, Judith Caseley, and Barbara Santucci all took the time and effort to pose for a special photograph. A special thank you to each of them.

A warm hug and a thank you to illustrator and culinary advisor Deborah L. McElmeel. Her sketches can be found on most pages in this book, and many of the recipes (those not submitted by the author or illustrator) were developed or adapted by her. Perhaps her Hot Marshmallow Cheesecake with Raspberry Fudge Sauce, developed to correspond with Jenny's celebration dessert in Steven Kellogg's *Island of the Skog,* is among Deborah's most delectable concoctions for this book. Another favorite are the Marco Polo bars in the chapter featuring Feeney.

Each of the food dishes are indexed so that you can find literary connections by the food; or you can find the author/illustrator and then find the food connection. Within each author/illustrator section we have included booklists for more reading and bits and facts about related topics. The indices include a combined theme/subject index and a recipe index. Sources for more information about the bits and facts are also appended at the end of the book.

Read, share, and enjoy.

Sharron L. McElmeel

David A. Adler—Birthday Cake

Photo: Nina Crews

David A. Adler

Birthday: April 10

Favorite place: his writing room

Favorite foods: blueberries and ginger

Family:

    Spouse—Renee Hamada (a school psychologist)

    Sons—Michael, Eddie, Eitan, and a daughter-in-law, Deborah

Home:

    Childhood—Lawrence, NY

    Now—Woodmere, NY

I was always the "creative one." I was a cartoonist before I was a writer. I was a math teacher, arts and crafts teacher, and a waiter, too.

—David A. Adler

David A. Adler grew up in a large family —his brothers, Eddie, Joseph, and Nathan, and his sisters, Caroline and Susan, were always encouraged to be individuals. David was known as a dreamer. He was an artist and often used his pictures to help him think up stories to tell his younger siblings. Many of the ideas for his fiction writing come from his memories of childhood. He actually based the character of Eric in the Cam Jansen series on himself. His fiction usually begins with the character. His nonfiction emerges from subjects he is curious about.

An incident on one of his birthdays during his childhood inadvertently taught him a lot about writing in general.

"Many years ago, for my birthday, my mom baked a cake. Since it was my birthday, Mom gave me the first slice.

"I tasted it and said, 'This cake tastes terrible.'

"Mom said, 'No, it doesn't. I've made this cake lots of times and you always love it. Take another bite.'

" 'Take another bite!' I said. 'Why would I take another bite if the first bite is so bad?'

"For me, that seems a perfect analogy for my writing.

"I try to make my first sentence of my fiction—my cake—terrific, so my readers will keep reading—will take another bite.

"I'm sure you are wondering why I said the cake tasted terrible. Mom tasted it and said, 'It does taste funny. I wonder why.'

"She tasted the ingredients, the butter, flour, and sugar and then asked, 'Who put the salt in the sugar?'

"My sister had. She ruined the cake, but taught me about writing. I learned to start my stories with a great first sentence."

—David A. Adler

1

BIRTHDAY CAKES AND CELEBRATIONS

In the days of the great Egyptian rulers, only their birthdays, and those of no one else, were celebrated. There were parades and circuses, and much food. The early Romans had parades and chariot races—but usually for their gods. The birthdays of mere mortals were of little importance.

It is said to have been in Germany that birthday cakes were first made a little over two hundred years ago—sweetened bread dough covered with sugar.

Mystery Writer's Cake

This cake has a mystery ingredient (tomato soup) and also leaves out some ingredients that are normally included in cakes. Those who enjoy eating the cake might also wonder what is and is not in the cake. The cake has no eggs, butter, or milk—a great recipe for friends with allergies to those ingredients.

In a large mixing bowl combine and beat until fluffy:

- 1 cup sugar
- 2 tablespoons shortening

Sift together (in a second bowl):

- 2 cups flour
- 1/2 teaspoon salt
- 1 teaspoon cinnamon
- 1/2 teaspoon cloves
- 1/2 teaspoon nutmeg
- 1 teaspoon soda

Stir the sifted ingredients in about three parts into the sugar mixture alternately with thirds of one can of canned tomato soup (10.5-ounce size).

Beat the batter until it is smooth after each addition. Fold in:

- 1 cup nut meats (optional)
- 1 cup raisins (optional)

Bake the cake in a greased 9-inch tube pan in a moderate oven (350° F) for about 45 minutes.

Birthday Cake Supreme

Beat together until creamy:

- 1/2 cup vegetable oil or melted butter
- 1 cup sugar
- 1 egg
- 4 egg yolks

When all graininess disappears, add:

- 1 teaspoon orange extract
- 1/3 teaspoon salt

Sift together:

- 1 1/2 cups flour
- 1/4 cup cornstarch
- 2 1/2 teaspoons baking powder

Add to the sugar and egg mixture:

1/3 of the flour mixture, then 1/4 cup milk

Beat

Add another 1/3 of the flour mixture, then 1/4 cup milk

Beat

Add final 1/3 of the flour mixture

Beat until the batter is smooth and creamy.

Put batter in a lightly greased tube pan and bake 45 minutes in a moderately hot oven, 350° to 375° F. Cool, brush off the crumbs, and decorate with your favorite frosting/icing. Fill the "hole" in the center with tiny favors or with fresh flowers. Put the cake on a small tray covered with a paper doily; add a decorated edge of fresh flowers or a piped border of frosting.

Selected Books Written by David A. Adler

David A. Adler has written more than 170 books since his first was published in 1977, while he was on child-care leave from his teaching position after the birth of his first son, Michael. His books fit into several categories, such as mystery and detective stories including series with Cam Jansen, Andy Russell, and Jeffrey Bones; Holocaust books; picture book biographies; math and riddle books; and many other fiction and information books.

Bones and the Cupcake Mystery. Illustrated by Barbara Johansen Newman. (Viking, 2005)

Bones and the Dinosaur Mystery. Illustrated by Barbara Johansen Newman. (Viking, 2005)

Cam Jansen and the Mystery of the Babe Ruth Baseball. Illustrated by Susanna Natti. (Viking, 2004)

A Hero and the Holocaust: The Story of Janusz Korczak and His Children. Illustrated by Bill Farnsworth. (Holiday House, 2002)

Hiding from the Nazis. Illustrated by Karen Ritz. (Holiday House, 1997)

It's a Baby, Andy Russell. Illustrated by Leanne Franson. (Harcourt, 2005)

Joe Louis: America's Fighter. Illustrated by Terry Widener. (Harcourt, 2005)

Mama Played Baseball. Illustrated by Chris O'Leary. (Harcourt/Gulliver, 2003)

Young Cam Jansen and the Substitute Mystery. Illustrated by Susanna Natti. (Viking, 2005)

Baking Mishaps

Amato, William. *Math in the Kitchen.* (Children's Press, 2002)—math used in making brownies.

Beck, Andrea. *Elliot Bakes a Cake.* (An Elliot Moose Story). (Kids Can Press, 1999)—mishaps can be fixed.

Christelow, Eileen. *Don't Wake Up Mama!* (Clarion, 1992)—five little monkeys make their mother a birthday cake.

Sachar, Louis. *Flying Birthday Cake?* (Random House, 1999)—funny

Van Hichtum, Nienke. *Apple Cake.* (Floris Books, 1996)—a woman sets off to get enough apples to bake a cake.

Laurie Halse Anderson—Cranberry Jell-O

Thanksgiving sums up everything I love in the world; family, and the spirit of thankfulness.

—Laurie Halse Anderson

Laurie Halse Anderson

Birthday: October 23

Favorite place: Home with my family or hiking in the woods

Favorite foods: Popcorn, pumpkin pie—all Thanksgiving food!

Family:

Spouse—Scot Larrabee

Son—Christian Larrabee

Daughters—Jessica Larrabee, Meredith Anderson, Stephanie Anderson

Home state:

Childhood—northern New York State

Now—northern New York State

When I was a little girl, Thanksgiving was spent at my grandparents in the mountains, with aunts, uncles, and cousins. My grandparents always seemed like magical creatures to me, wise and merry. I hope their spirit comes through in *Turkey Pox.*

I loved researching and writing my second literacy celebration of Thanksgiving, *Thank You, Sarah!* Sarah Hale and I share several Yankee ancestors in common. We are also both patriotic Americans, believers in the power of the pen, and big fans of roast turkey and mashed potatoes.

Other culinary tidbits and crumbs can be found scattered in my work for older readers. You'll find another Thanksgiving scene and significant Ho-Ho in *Speak,* doughnuts, Jell-O, and chicken and biscuits served up in *Catalyst,* and in my novel, *Prom,* be on the look-out for canned ravioli.

—Laurie Halse Anderson

Booklist

Selected Books Written by Laurie Halse Anderson

Catalyst. (Viking, 2002; Young Adult)

Fever, 1793. (Simon & Schuster, 2000; Young Adult)

Nedito Runs. Illustrated by Anita Van Der Merwe. (Henry Holt & Co., 1996)

Prom. (Viking, 2005)

Race to the Finish (Wild at Heart #12). (Pleasant Company, 2003)

Speak. (Farrar, Straus & Giroux, 1999; Young Adult)

Thank You, Sarah! The Woman Who Saved Thanksgiving. Illustrated by Matt Faulkner. (Simon & Schuster, 2002)

Turkey Pox. Illustrated by Dorothy Donohue. (Whitman, 1996)

THANKSGIVING DINNER

According to numerous articles written by historians at the Plimouth Colony Living History Museum and Kathleen A. Curtin, food historian, our contemporary dinner of turkey, mashed potatoes, and cranberry sauce probably would not have been part of the food served at the traditional first Thanksgiving. Hunters would have brought back venison and fowl—probably duck and geese for the feast. Cranberries were available, but it would be fifty years before mention is made of boiling them with sugar to make a sauce to eat with meat. Pumpkin and squash would have been available, but pies as we know them would not have been.

The pumpkin and squash would likely have been roasted. Many berries and food from their gardens would have been available: parsnips, collards, carrots, parsley, turnips, spinach, cabbages, sage, thyme, marjoram, and onions, along with cultivated beans and dried wild blueberries, grapes, and nuts.

Sara Josepha Hale (October 24, 1788–April 30, 1879)

Sara Josepha Hale was a writer and editor. Two of her best-known contributions are the verse "Mary Had a Little Lamb" and her advocacy for establishing Thanksgiving Day as a national holiday. She used her magazine to write pro-Thanksgiving articles and wrote hundreds of letters. President Abraham Lincoln signed the first proclamation, in 1863, for an annual day of national thanksgiving.

Pumpkin Pizzazz Roll

- 3 eggs, beaten
- 1 cup sugar
- 2/3 cup canned pumpkin (or fresh pumpkin)
- 3/4 cup flour
- 1 teaspoon baking soda
- 1 teaspoon nutmeg
- 2 teaspoons cinnamon
- 1/2 teaspoon cloves

Beat eggs and sugar until creamy. Add in remaining ingredients. Beat until smooth. Pour batter onto a greased jelly-roll pan; bake at 350F for 10 to 15 minutes.

Place a clean dish towel over the cake. Invert pan onto a kitchen towel. Roll up the cake in the towel, jelly-roll style, to cool. While the cake is cooling, make the filling.

Combine and beat until smooth and fluffy:

- 8 ounces cream cheese, softened
- 1/2 cup powdered sugar
- 1/4 cup butter, softened
- 1 teaspoon vanilla

Unroll cooled cake and spread filling over cake. Reroll the cake. Optional: Add a little milk to a 1/4 cup of the filling, just enough to make the filling slide down the sides of the log when you spread the filling over the top of the log. Sprinkle crushed walnuts onto the top side of the frosted log. Store in refrigerator. Serve as a log with a decorative knife for people to slice off their own serving, or slice in 1-inch slices and arrange on a platter.

Learn about Cranberries

Check your local library for these titles.

Burns, Diane L. *Cranberries: Fruit of the Bogs.* Illustrated by Cheryl Walsh Bellville. (Carolrhoda, 1994)

Jaspersohn, William. *Cranberries.* (Houghton Mifflin, 1991)

Snyder, Inez. *Cranberries.* (Children's Press, 2004)

Cranberries and Jell-O

Three fruits are native to North America: cranberries, blueberries, and Concord grapes. The cranberry was eaten by Native Americans in many forms: fresh, ground, or mashed with cornmeal and baked into bread. They often dried the berries with wild game to make a ration for long trips or to sustain them during long, difficult winters. Later when maple sugar and honey were available, these were used to sweeten the berries. The cranberry (although that was a name, "crane-berry," given by the Pilgrims) was a staple of the Native Americans long before the Pilgrims arrived on the continent.

Cranberries have become a mainstay of today's Thanksgiving dinner. Our Cranberry Jell-O recipe incorporates one of Laurie Halse Anderson's favorite foods, Jell-O, with the cranberry to mix the traditional with the more modern (gelatin was first used in 1897 and did not become popular until the middle 1900s).

Cranberry Jell-O

Pour a 20-ounce can of crushed pineapple into a bowl and heat (in a microwave or a pan) until the liquid boils. This inactivates the enzymes in the pineapple.

Drain the crushed pineapple from the juice and use the juice as part of the liquid used to prepare two large packages of Cranberry (or Strawberry) Jell-O as directed on the carton. Include the juice in the allocation of liquid to be used. Overall use 1/2 cup less liquid than the directions specify.

Into the liquid Jell-O combine:

- 2 cups whole fresh or frozen cranberries, chopped
- Crushed pineapple, previously heated and drained
- 1 package frozen or fresh raspberries
- 1 cup walnut pieces (not crushed)

Put mixture in mold or serving bowl and put in refrigerator to chill and set.

Caroline Arnold—Anasazi Bean Soup

Anasazi beans were very much like to-day's pinto beans. The Anasazi ate them fresh and also dried them to be used later.

—from *The Ancient Cliff Dwellers of Mesa Verde* by Caroline Arnold

Caroline Arnold

Birthday: May 16

Favorite place: Mesa Verde is one of my favorite places—I particularly like to visit places where people lived in prehistoric times.

Favorite foods: Soups, breads, desserts.

Family:

    Spouse—Arthur Arnold (a neuroscientist)

    Son—Matthew (a neurologist)

    Daughter—Jennifer (a linguist); grandchildren: Alessanda and Lucas

Home:

    Childhood—Born in Pittsburgh, spent childhood in Minneapolis, Minnesota

    Now—Los Angeles, California

Caroline Arnold was born in Pittsburgh, Pennsylvania, but at the age of four her family moved to Minneapolis where she spent the rest of her childhood. One summer, the year she was fourteen, she says her family "went on an extended summer camping trip from our home in Minnesota to Southern California. One of the highlights along the way was a visit to Mesa Verde National Park in southwestern Colorado. At that time, the campground was on top of the mesa, just a stone's throw from the visitor center and the ruins of Spruce Tree House. My brothers and I spent hours climbing the ladders and exploring the ruins. Inside the visitor center I loved peering at the dioramas with their tiny houses and people, and reading about the pottery, tools, and other items in the exhibit cases, trying to imagine what life was like when the Anasazi had inhabited these mesas and canyons. In the evening, our family cooked our meal and ate it around the campfire, much as Anasazi families must have done more than a thousand years ago."

Years later when Arnold wrote *The Ancient Cliff Dwellers of Mesa Verde* she wrote that, because of its elevation, the Mesa Verde was slightly cooler and wetter than the plains below it. Combined with the rich soil, this climate made the Mesa a great place to raise crops. Sometime during a two-hundred-year period, from A.D. 550 to 750, beans became an important source of protein in the Anasazi diet.

During visits to Mesa Verde with photographer Richard Hewett, while researching her book about the ancient cliff dwellers, Arnold found the park just as fascinating as she had as a child. She said, "One of my favorite parts of the park was a small garden plot near the visitor center where the park rangers were growing corn, squash, and beans, just as the Anasazi had in prehistoric times."

Arnold was delighted when she found a recipe for Anasazi Bean Soup, and although she says, "I doubt that the ancient Anasazi used ham hocks or lemon in their recipes, I can imagine that they might have put a chunk of deer meat and locally gathered flavorings into their beans as they cooked them over the fire."

Photo: Richard Hewitt

The Anasazi bean is named after an extinct ancient Native American tribe. The Anasazi are thought to have left their homes in the late A.D. 1200s, but more than 750 years later (in 1950), archeologists uncovered a clay pot with some dried beans inside. Some say these beans sprouted and became the source of all modern Anasazi beans, but seed specialists doubt if this could be true. Nonetheless, another legend has it that the first settlers found beans growing wild, and later archeologists found the same beans in an ancient clay pot. The beans were first sold commercially around 1983.

The Anasazi bean is white with a maroon pattern. Although related to the pinto bean, the Anasazi bean is more flavorful, sweeter, and easier to digest. It also is less prone to produce gas. Anasazi beans cook somewhat faster and can be substituted for pinto or red kidney beans in your favorite dishes.

The Anasazi

The mystery of the Anasazi Native Americans and their demise continues to intrigue many to this day. Find out more about the Anasazi.

The Lost World of the Anasazi: Exploring the Mysteries of Chaco Canyon by Peter Lourie. (Boyds Mills Press, 2003)

The Anasazi Culture at Mesa Verde (Events That Shaped America) by Sabrina Crewe. (Gareth Stevens Publishing, 2002)

Anasazi Beans

Many Native American tribes grow beans and now Anasazi beans are available commercially. After they are harvested, the beans are often dried and stored for later use. Beans were often served with corn or flour tortillas, as they still are today.

- 1 pound dried Anasazi beans
- 6 cups water
- 1/4 cup finely chopped onions
- 1 clove garlic, crushed
- 6 slices bacon, chopped
- 1/4 cup finely chopped green pepper

- 1 jalapeno, diced
- 1 teaspoon chili powder
- 1/2 teaspoon cumin
- 1/4 teaspoon cayenne powder
- Salt and pepper, to taste

Directions: In a skillet, sauté onion, pepper, garlic, and bacon. Reserve the sautéed ingredients. Combine the remaining ingredients in a saucepan. Boil for 1 to 1 1/2 hours or until the beans are very tender. Drain beans, reserving liquid. Add sautéed ingredients to the beans and mash together, adding liquid a little at a time, until mixture is smooth. Serve with tortillas or cornbread.

Anasazi Bean Soup

- 1 package of red, pinto type, beans
- 2 quarts of water
- 1 or 2 ham hocks
- Salt and pepper to taste
- 1 16 ounce can of tomatoes
- 1 large onion, chopped
- 1 clove garlic, minced
- 1 to 1 1/2 teaspoons chili powder
- Juice of 1/2 lemon

Soak beans overnight. Drain beans. Add water, ham, salt, and pepper. Cook until beans are tender. Add tomatoes, onion, garlic, and chili powder and cook another half hour. Add lemon juice just before serving.

Signature Recipe—Caroline Arnold

Booklist

Selected Books Written By Caroline Arnold

Ancient Cliff Dwellers of Mesa Verde. Illustrated with color photographs by Richard Hewett. (Clarion Books, 1992)

Birds: Nature's Magnificent Flying Machines. Illustrated by Patricia Wynne. (Charlesbridge, 2003)

Dinosaurs with Feathers. Illustrated by Laurie Caple. (Clarion Books, 2001)

Pterosaurs, Rulers of the Skies in the Dinosaur Age. Illustrated by Laurie Caple. (Clarion Books, 2004)

Uluru, Australia's Aboriginal Heart. Illustrated with photographs by Arthur Arnold. (Clarion Books, 2003)

When Mammoths Walked the Earth. Illustrated by Laurie Caple. (Clarion Books, 2002)

Who Has More? Who Has Fewer? Illustrated by Caroline Arnold. (Charlesbridge, 2004)

Who Is Bigger? Who Is Smaller? Illustrated by Caroline Arnold. (Charlesbridge, 2004)

Jim Aylesworth—Fudge

Photo: Sharron L. McElmeel

Watching my father at work in the kitchen, waiting to taste the test, helping to stir, licking the wooden spoon, and eating my father's fudge are some of the most pleasant memories of my childhood and of my father.

—Jim Aylesworth

Jim Aylesworth spent more than two decades in classrooms where he taught first graders and read them hundreds of books. Two of his favorite books were *The Sneetches* by Dr. Seuss and *The Tale of Peter Rabbit* by Beatrix Potter. Now he has authored the favorite books of many other readers. At first he wrote stories and read them to his first-grade students. His students encouraged him. He wrote stories that children wanted to read. He submitted the stories to publishers and received rejections—and more rejections. Still his students encouraged him. Finally his first book was accepted for publication, and after several years of teaching and writing, he retired from teaching first grade and became a full-time writer.

Aylesworth was born in Jacksonville, Florida, and spent his childhood in Alabama, Texas, and Indiana. His grandparents owned a farm in Hebron, Indiana, where Jim spent many of his younger days. In fact, one of his first books was *Hanna's Hog,* a book that was inspired by a legendary figure in the town's history. Hanna Brody died when Jim was a child, but he remembers that she lived in a little cabin and smoked a pipe—images that showed up in the book. Hanna kept chickens in a yard with no grass, and she would sweep the yard with a broom. Jim and his brother Bill now own the farm, and it is often the site of the brothers' family get-togethers.

Jim Aylesworth

Birthday: February 21

Favorite place: Indiana farm

Favorite foods: Fudge, sugar cookies, angel food cake

Family:

    Spouse—Donna

    Sons—John and Daniel

Home:

    Childhood—Born in Jacksonville, Florida; lived in Alabama, Texas, and Indiana

    Now—Chicago, Illinois

Jim talks about his life and his books in *Jim Aylesworth and You* (Libraries Unlimited, 2005). Written with Jennifer K. Rotole.

Although Aylesworth says, "I am much more into eating than into cooking," he does have two recipes that are important to him. The first one is his father's fudge recipe, and the second his great-grandmother's sugar cookie recipe, which was included on the back cover of *The Tale of Tricky Fox*. The original recipe, for the sugar cookies, called for lard to be used, but shortening was substituted in the printed recipe. He might have had a third recipe if he could have found it as he says, "My maternal grandmother made an oh so wonderful Angel Food cake."

Gingerbread People

- 1/3 cup shortening
- 1/3 cup brown sugar
- 1 egg
- 1/2 teaspoon vanilla
- 2/3 cup molasses

- 2 3/4 cup flour
- 1 teaspoon soda
- 1 teaspoon salt
- 2 teaspoons cinnamon
- 1 teaspoon ginger

Mix all ingredients. Knead into a soft ball and flatten. Roll out to 1/4-inch thickness. Use cookie cutter to cut out people shapes. Decorate with chocolate chips, cinnamon candies (e.g., Red Hots), or raisins, as desired. Bake at 350° F or until done, 8 to 10 minutes. Middle of the cookie will be puffy and soft but not wiggly when they are done. Cool on a rack.

FAMILY RECIPES

Favorite recipes are often associated with a favorite person or favorite stories. Aylesworth shares his father's fudge recipe here, mentions his great-grandmother's sugar cookie recipe (find it in Aylesworth's *The Tale of Tricky Fox*), and his maternal grandmother's angel food cake recipe. We've shared our favorite gingerbread recipe and connected it to Aylesworth's *The Gingerbread Man*. Gather together favorite recipes from members of your family; add a family story or two and create a story cookbook.

Norm's Chocolate Fudge

- 2 cups sugar
- 1/2 cup milk
- 1/3 cup white corn syrup (e.g., Karo brand)
- 2 squares of unsweetened chocolate

Mix together in a cooking pot.

Set at medium heat, and bring to a boil (about 10 minutes).

Continue cooking, stirring occasionally, until the candy reaches a rolling boil.

Testing to see whether the mixture is done:

Test in cold water. Put an ice cube in 2 cups of water.

Drop a small amount of the boiling mixture into the water and stir with fingers until the drops come together into a soft ball. Generally, two or three tests are necessary. Eat every test!!

When the test is OK, remove from the heat and set the pot to cool in cool water in the sink (about 10 minutes).

Add:

- 1 teaspoon vanilla
- 1 tablespoon butter
- 1 pinch of salt
- 1 dash of cinnamon

Stir-beat until the fudge loses its gloss and becomes stiff (15–25 minutes).

Pour into a buttered platter and cut into squares.

Signature Recipe—Jim Aylesworth

Norm's Chocolate Fudge Coconut Balls

Have ready several large marshmallows, cut in half, and a dish of coconut for rolling the fudge balls. Prepare the fudge the same as Norm's Chocolate Fudge; however, let the test be a little bit stiffer. Beat longer. The fudge should still be warm (hot), but workable.

Wash and butter your hands.

Put half a marshmallow into the fudge pan. With a spoon, scoop out enough of the mixture to cover the marshmallow. Roll the scoop into a ball, and roll the ball in the coconut. Work fast and repeat the process until all the fudge is scooped around a marshmallow. It helps if two people work at a time.

Signature Recipe—Jim Aylesworth

Selected Books Written by Jim Aylesworth

The Burger and the Hot Dog. Illustrated by Stephen Gammell. (Atheneum, 2002)

The Gingerbread Man. Illustrated by Barbara McClintock. (Scholastic, 1998)

Goldilocks and the Three Bears. Illustrated by Barbara McClintock. (Scholastic, 2003)

Hanna's Hog. Illustrated by Glen Rounds. (Atheneum, 1988)

My Son John. Illustrated by David Frampton. (Henry Holt, 1994)

Old Black Fly. Illustrated by Stephen Gammell. (Henry Holt, 1992)

The Tale of Tricky Fox. Illustrated by Barbara McClintock. (Scholastic, 2001)

Gingerbread Books

Amoss, Berthe. *Cajun Gingerbread Boy.* (MTC Press, 1999)

Aylesworth, Jim. *The Gingerbread Man.* Illustrated by Barbara McClintock. (Scholastic, 1998)

Brett, Jan. *Gingerbread Baby.* (Putnam, 1999)

Cook, Scott. *The Gingerbread Boy.* (Dragonfly, 1996; paperback)

Egielski, Richard. *The Gingerbread Boy.* (HarperCollins, 1997; set in an urban city; includes a recipe)

Galdone, Paul. *The Gingerbread Boy.* (Clarion, 1979)

Kimmel, Eric. *The Gingerbread Man.* Illustrated by Megan Lloyd. (Holiday House, 1994; variant ending has gingerbread people returning each time someone bakes a batch)

Mary Azarian—Cinnamon Rolls

Photo: John Guare

I was born into a family that loved to cook. My maternal grandmother ran a "lunch-room" in Washington, D.C., and her cooking was legendary.... My father's mother lived near us and cared for me while my mother worked. She was a fabulous baker and my earliest memories are of her kitchen where she worked wonders.

—Mary Azarian

Mary Azarian

Birthday: December 8

Favorite place: Vermont

Favorite foods: anything lemon—pies, bars, lemon curd; macaroni and cheese, homemade pizza, Yorkshire pudding, artisan breads

Family:

   Sons—Ethan, Tim, and Jesse

Home:

   Childhood—Vermont

   Now—Vermont; her sons live in Austin, Texas (Ethan), and in Oakland, California (Tim and Jesse). All three are involved in the arts.

For more than forty years Mary Azarian cooked and baked and created her artwork on a small hill farm in Vermont. She raised three sons and became a renowned illustrator of children's books. In the 1990s, she moved her art studio to an old farmhouse where her Macintosh computer sits side-by-side with the nineteenth-century press that she still uses. She is also an avid gardener and baker, no doubt in part because her beloved paternal grandmother was an avid gardener and baker.

"I especially remember the smell of yeast dough rising and cinnamon rolls baking. My mother, also a good cook, disliked sweets and never made desserts. My father and I both had a sweet tooth and I became the family baker at the age of seven with my first pie. It was a lemon pie with a top crust! I don't remember that pie, but somehow the family got it down and I was encouraged to continue with my efforts. My repertoire expanded to include all sorts of cakes, pies, cookies and puddings, but I never ventured into the waters of yeast baking.

Illustration credit: © 2004, Mary Azarian, from Miss Bridie Chose a Shovel.

"After moving to Vermont in the 1960s my partner and I became 'back-to-the-landers' on a small hill farm. It seemed a necessary part of subsistence living to bake bread. As I kneaded my first dough, memories of Grandma's kitchen came flooding back. At the height of my bread-baking career, I was making twenty-five loaves a week for my growing family. With freshly churned butter and homemade jam, the bread was irresistible, especially hot from the oven. Much as my family enjoyed the loaves of bread that came from the big wood burning range, their favorite treat was the cinnamon rolls that I baked for special occasions."

—Mary Azarian

BAKING CINNAMON ROLLS
(ABOUT THE RECIPE AND METHOD)

I long ago ceased to measure when making yeast doughs. You get a feel for what's needed after several thousand batches of bread, rolls etc. So this recipe (Mary Azarian's Cinnamon Rolls) has room for a lot of variations. The dough recipe I've given here makes a rich dough. You can leave out the egg and some of the oil and still get a good result. You can add any kind of nut you like, and many people like raisins, dried cherries, or dried cranberries. Play around with the amount of flour, just be sure not to make the dough too stiff.

—Mary Azarian

If you can, buy the baking yeast at a local food co-op. It's a lot cheaper than the packets you get in the supermarket. Store it in the refrigerator for up to six months.

Mary Azarian's Cinnamon Rolls

- 1 cup scalded milk
- 1/2 cup warm water
- 1 egg
- 1 teaspoon salt
- 1 tablespoon dry baking yeast
- 3 tablespoons melted butter or safflower oil
- 2 tablespoons sugar, honey, or maple syrup
- Enough flour to make a soft dough, about 4 cups

Dissolve the dry yeast in the water and milk. Stir in the other ingredients along with the flour and turn out onto a floured board, or preferably a marble slab. Knead until the dough is smooth and stretchy, about 10 minutes. Brush a large bowl with oil, place dough in the bowl and turn it to coat the dough with the oil and then cover the bowl with plastic wrap. Leave in a warm place to double in bulk.

Preheat the oven to 375° F. Melt 1 stick of butter in a 9 x 13–inch baking pan and sprinkle 1 cup brown sugar and 1 cup chopped pecans over the melted butter. Set the pan aside and return to the dough.

Place the dough on the floured surface and roll into a long rectangle approximately 1/4 inch thick. Brush the dough with a little melted butter and sprinkle with cinnamon to taste. Roll up the dough like a jelly roll and cut the roll into 1-inch rounds. Place them on top of the butter, sugar, nut combination, making sure they are close together. Let rise again until doubled in bulk and bake for approximately 25 minutes or until they are lightly browned. Be careful not to overbake. Turn the pan out onto a large platter as soon as you remove it from the oven. You can serve the rolls as is or gild the lily with a simple icing made from 1/4 cup soft butter, 1 tablespoon cream, 1 teaspoon pure vanilla extract, and enough confectioner's sugar to make a soft mixture. Spread the icing on the rolls while still warm. The rolls are best eaten immediately, but no one will turn them down if that's not possible.

Signature Recipe—Mary Azarian

Selected Books Illustrated by Mary Azarian

A Christmas Like Helen's. Text by Natalie Kinsey-Warnock. (Houghton Mifflin, 2004)

Darrell. Text by Leda Schubert. (Houghton Mifflin, 2005)

From Dawn till Dusk. Text by Natalie Kinsey-Warnock. (Houghton Mifflin, 2002)

A Gardener's Alphabet. Text by Mary Azarian. (Houghton Mifflin, 2000)

Louisa May & Mr. Thoreau's Flute. Text by Julie Dunlap & Marybeth Lorbiecki. (Dial Books for Young Readers, 2002)

Miss Bridie Chose a Shovel. Text by Leslie Connor. (Houghton Mifflin, 2004)

Snowflake Bentley. Text by Jacqueline Briggs Martin. (Houghton Mifflin, 1999)

Bob Barner—Pecan Pie

Photo: Sharron L. McElmeel

Growing up in northern Ohio with southern parents I could never understand why some of our meals were so different from those of my friends. Southern fried chicken was great but the black-eyed peas and okra were definitely weird. One of the things I always liked was my Mother's pecan pie.

—Bob Barner

Bob Barner

Birthday: November 11

Favorite place: Venice, Italy

Favorite foods: Cajun and Japanese (go figure!)

Family:

Parents—Father, Joe; Mother, Jean

Spouse—Catherine Barner

Home:

Childhood—Arkansas (for the first two weeks), then Eastlake, Ohio

Now—San Francisco, California

In Bob Barner's books readers can find information about bones, maps, bugs, dinosaurs, stars, and elephants. He writes about things that interest him, and he manages to make the information-filled books full of rhythm and movement—through pictures and words. Barner creates his illustrations with pen, ink, and watercolor as well as cut and torn paper. The colors he uses are always bold and dynamic.

Bob Barner talks about his life and books in *Bob Barner and You* (Libraries Unlimited, 2006).

Bob Barner was born in Tuckerman, Arkansas, but his family soon moved to Ohio where he spent most of his childhood. After graduating from Columbus College of Art and Design in Columbus, Ohio, Barner embarked on a career in art. He designed educational publications, helped draw the Lil' Abner comic strip, worked in advertising agencies and at the Boston Museum of Science before becoming a full-time author and illustrator of books.

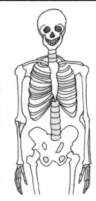

Skeleton Books

Barner's *Dem Bones* is a book filled with music and melody. His skeleton band supplies words and music to the well-known song based on the African American spiritual. Children will enjoy learning about the human body and having their funny bones tickled at the same time. Sing the song and read more books about bones and skeletons.

Anderson, Karen C., and Stephen Cumbaa. *The Bones & Skeleton Game Book* (Hand in Hand with Nature). (Workman Publishing, 1993)

Balestrino, Philip. *The Skeleton Inside You* (Let's-Read-and-Find-Out Science 2). (Harpertrophy, 1989)

Cumbaa, Stephen. *The Bones Book: Book and Skeleton* (Hand in Hand with Nature). (Workman Publishing, 1992; includes a moveable 12-inch, 25-piece skeleton model)

Llewellyn, Claire, and Peter Geissler. *The Big Book of Bones*. (Peter Bedrick Books, 2001)

Sandeman, Anna, et al. *Bones* (Body Books). (Copper Beech Books, 1995)

Simon, Seymour. *Bones: Our Skeletal System*. (Harpertrophy, 2000)

Weiner, Esther. *The Incredible Human Body*. (Scholastic, 1999)

Pecan Facts

Pecans are the only tree nuts native to North America, and they are particularly plentiful in the Southern states. Pecans were a major source of food for Native Americans as far back as the 1500s. Presidents George Washington and Thomas Jefferson grew pecan trees in their gardens. In 1919, the pecan tree was named the state tree of Texas. The production of pecans is a major industry in the southeastern United States. Eighty percent of the world's pecans are produced in the United States. Georgia is the leading pecan-producing state in the country, with nearly 55 million pounds of fresh pecans harvested in the fall of 2003. Okmulgee, Georgia, holds the world record for the largest pecan pie, pecan cookie, and pecan brownie. An annual pecan festival is held in Okmulgee each June. Albany, Georgia, is the site of the annual National Pecan Festival. As many as 600,000 pecan trees are growing in Albany—sometimes called the Pecan Capital of the United States. Because of modern-day grafting techniques there are now more than a thousand varieties of pecans.

Bob Barner's mom has a pecan tree in her backyard, and Bob says, "Today she bakes [pecan] pies with the nuts from her own tree. Not only is the tree home to numerous squirrels, magpies, and a family of robins, but it also produces delicious pecans."

Chicken—Southern Pecan Bake

This recipe is not the traditional fried chicken recipe, but it is a tasty variation of baked chicken that incorporates the nutty flavor of pecans and the crunchiness of fried chicken.

Pound 8 boneless and skinless chicken breasts to tenderize and thin.

Dissolve 6 teaspoons salt in 6 cups of ice water and then use the saltwater to marinate the chicken breasts for a half hour. Add ice cubes to keep the water very cold.

Grind pecans to make 1 cup pecan meal.

- 4 whole eggs
- 3 tablespoons milk
- 3 tablespoons honey
- 1/2 teaspoon salt
- 1/2 teaspoon fresh black pepper, coarsely ground

Beat milk and honey together, then add beaten eggs. Add salt and pepper. Put egg mixture in a shallow bowl. Put pecan meal in a second shallow bowl.

Dip each chicken breast in the egg wash, then into the pecan meal, and pat the meal into the breast to form a crust. Place the breasts in a shallow baking pan that has been sprayed with cooking spray, and bake for 35 minutes at 375° F, or until the breasts are done through.

Serve on a bed of wild rice with a green salad. Serves 8.

Southern Pecan Pie

- 3 eggs
- 1/2 cup sugar
- 1/4 teaspoon salt
- 1 cup light corn syrup
- 1 cup fresh pecan halves
- 1 teaspoon vanilla extract
- 1/4 cup melted butter
- 8-inch unbaked piecrust

Beat the eggs. Add sugar, salt, vanilla, syrup, and butter. Spread pecans on bottom of the pastry, flat side down. Pour mixture over the nuts. Make a fluted design in the edge of the crust with your fingers or a fork.

Place on the center rack of the oven. Bake at 450° F for 10 minutes. Lower temperature to 350° F and bake for another 35 minutes.

Signature Recipe—Bob Barner

Books Written/Illustrated by Bob Barner

Bug Safari. Written and illustrated by Bob Barner. (Holiday House, 2004)

Dem Bones. Written and illustrated by Bob Barner. (Chronicle Books, 1996)

Dinosaur Bones. Written and illustrated by Bob Barner. (Chronicle Books, 2001)

Fish Wish. Written and illustrated by Bob Barner. (Holiday House, 2000)

Parade Day. Written and illustrated by Bob Barner. (Holiday House, 2003)

Stars! Stars! Stars! Written and illustrated by Bob Barner. (Chronicle Books, 2002)

Where Crocodiles Have Wings. Text by Patricia C. McKissack. Illustrated by Bob Barner. (Holiday House, 2005)

Raymond Bial—German Potato Salad

I was most fascinated by Grandma's kitchen and Grandpa's garden.

—Raymond Bial

Raymond Bial has written more than eighty books, photo essays about myriad topics, from the Amish, to tenement life, to ghosts. He and his wife, Linda, earned graduate degrees in Library and Information Science, in 1979, from the University of Illinois. Later they settled in Urbana, Illinois, where Ray began a long career as a reference librarian at Parkland College. Away from Parkland he became a renowned photographer and writer. Raymond and Linda Bial make their home in Urbana with two of their three children, Sarah and Luke. Their older daughter, Anna, is a fashion designer living in New York.

Raymond Bial

Birthday: November 5

Favorite place: Home—although he loves to travel in North America (Alaska, Montana, and the Southwest—especially New Mexico and Arizona)

Favorite foods: Especially likes seafood—but likes to cookout flank steak with his own "secret" marinade.

Family:

    Spouse—Linda

    Son—Luke

    Daughters—Anna and Sarah

Home:

    Childhood—born in Illinois; and childhood homes in Montana, Washington, Indiana, Michigan, and Illinois

    Now—Urbana, Illinois

Visiting My Grandparents by Raymond Bial

I always loved visiting my grandparents' home. Every odor of their white clapboard house was to be inhaled, especially the distinctive blend of kitchen and garden. Always old to me, Grandma kept her grey hair pinned up. I just loved to inhale the fragrance of her hair as I snuggled within the warm folds of her polka dot dress. And I vividly remember her cooking in her kitchen, muttering in her native German, amid clouds of flour.

She had previously earned a living as a cook for a wealthy family. My grandfather once worked as a gardener on the same estate, and that was where they met. Raised on a small farm in Slovenia, my grandfather loved to grow flowers for their delightful beauty and delicious vegetables for the family table. All the lettuce, tomatoes, potatoes, onions, and green peppers were grown in his backyard plots. They purchased other ingredients at the neighborhood Piggly Wiggly grocery store.

My grandfather continued to tend his garden for nearly two decades after Grandma died until his own death just before spring planting in 1979. As it turned out, my mother died a year later, and I inherited my grandfather's tools through her: spade, hoe, shovels, and rakes, mysterious in their age and simplicity. I now work with these tools in my own backyard, and I still feel my grandfather's grip in the handles gleaming with a fine patina that match the calluses of his hands.

All of my children's books are inspired by loved ones, so it was only natural that I dedicated *A Handful of Dirt* to my grandparents.

Raymond's Dill Pickles

Bial adapted the following recipe to suit the taste of his own family. He says, these pickles are especially enjoyed by Sarah, and Luke and myself. Luke, in particular, loves these pickles so much that he has come to be widely known as pickleboy among his friends in the neighborhood. If I get a good crop, I make the pickles with cucumbers grown in my own backyard, just as my grandparents had a garden for more than sixty years. My wife Linda supplies the dill and bay leaves from her herb garden in our backyard.

- 10 to 12 medium-sized cucumbers (each 3 to 4 inches long)
- 3 or 4 dill heads
- 1 cup white vinegar
- 4 or 5 garlic cloves, chopped
- 8 cups water
- 3 tablespoons pickling spice
- 1/4 cup pickling salt
- 2 bay leaves

Boil water, vinegar, and pickling salt in a stainless-steel sauce pan. Allow the liquid to cool while preparing other ingredients.

Place dill heads, chopped garlic, pickling spice, and bay leaves in a 1-gallon glass jar.

Thoroughly wash cucumbers, trim ends, and place in the jar. Cucumbers may be cut into chunks to fit more into the jar.

Carefully pour cooled liquid into the jar.

Place in refrigerator. Pickles are ready in four days. They must be kept refrigerated and will keep for weeks, but in our house they are usually gone within a week or two.

Signature Recipe—Raymond Bial

German Potato Salad

This recipe was originally Bial's great-grandmother recipe from the old country. Bial says, "I am pleased to have this recipe, written in my mother's own hand." Traditionally served on Easter with ham on his grandmother's cherished blue platter that was handed down to Bial through his mother.

- 6 or 7 large potatoes, diced
- 1 onion, chopped
- 1 small jar of red pimentos
- 1 green bell pepper, diced
- 1/2 pound bacon
- 1 or 2 tablespoons flour
- 1 or 2 tablespoons sugar
- 1/2 cup vinegar
- 1/4 cup water
- 1/4 teaspoon pepper

Boil diced potatoes until just tender. Drain and put aside.

Fry bacon in large skillet until crisp. Remove bacon and allow to cool briefly. Drain the bacon grease, leaving a little in the pan. Crumble bacon in the pan, along with diced onion, green pepper, water, vinegar, flour, and sugar. Stir until these ingredients thicken into a light gravy. Add red pimentos.

Add more or less sugar and vinegar to taste, which should be tangy like Chinese hot and sour dishes. Place the potatoes in a large bowl. Pour gravy mixture over potatoes and lightly toss. There should also be enough of the sauce to cover the potatoes thoroughly. I often vary the ingredients, adding more water, vinegar, flour, and sugar to obtain a little more sauce.

Avoid skimping on the sauce. It flavors the potatoes better to have a little too much than not enough. Serve warm.

Signature Recipe—Raymond Bial

Selected Books Written/Illustrated by Raymond Bial

Cow Towns (American Community Series). (Children's Press, 2004)

The Delawares (Lifeways Series). (Benchmark Books, 2004)

Ghost Towns of the American West. (Historical and Old West) (Houghton Mifflin, 2001)

A Handful of Dirt. (Walker, 2000)

The Long Walk: The Story of Navajo Captivity. (Great Journeys Series) (Benchmark Books, 2002)

Tenement: Immigrant Life on the Lower East Side. (Houghton Mifflin, 2002)

Underground Railroad. (Random House, 1998)

Where Washington Walked. (Walker, 2005)

With Needle and Thread: A Book about Quilts. (Houghton Mifflin, 1996)

Dirt and Compost—Gardening

Bial, Raymond. *A Handful of Dirt.* (Walker, 2000)

Christian, Peggy. *If You Find a Rock.* (Harcourt, 2000)

Cronin, Doreen. *Diary of a Worm.* (Joanna Cotler, 2003)

Himmelman, John. *An Earthworm's Life.* (Nature Upclose) (Children's Press, 2001)

Lavies, Bianca. *Compost Critters.* (Dutton, 1993)

Nancarrow, Loren. *The Worm Book: The Complete Guide to Worms in Your Garden.* (Ten Speed Press, 1998)

Robbins, Ken. *Earth.* (Holt, 1995)

Schmid, Eleonore. *The Living Earth.* (North-South, 1994)

Silverstein, Alvin, and Virginia Silverstein. *Life in a Bucket of Soil.* (Dover, 2000)

Tomecek, Steve. *Dirt: Jump Into Science* (Jump into Science). (National Geographic, 2002)

Ashley Bryan—Sweet Potato Pie

Photo Credit: Sharron L. McElmeel

Do you know my granny's name?
Will you tell it to me plain?
I won't get bread pudding
Or sweet-potato pie
Until I tell her real name to her,
Saying "Granny" just won't do her.

—from *Turtle Knows Your Name*
by Ashley Bryan

Ashley Bryan

Birthday: July 13

Favorite place: Islesford, Maine

Favorite foods: Fungi, sweet potato pie, bread pudding

Family:

   Siblings: Three brothers and two sisters, including Elaine Martindale.

Home:

   Childhood—Bronx, New York City

   Now—Lives in Cranberry Isles, on Islesford (sometimes called Little Cranberry) off the coast of Maine near Bangor.

Years ago while a college student, Ashley Bryan discovered a small island, Islesford, off the coast of Maine. Islesford was a small remote fishing village in the Cranberry Isles. He had grown up in the Bronx, where he returned, after serving in the military and earning his college degree, in 1950. For many years he taught at Queens College and worked at his art in his studio. Since childhood he had made books for friends and family. That continued into his adult life. Soon he was invited to submit some work to a publisher. He did, and his first book was published in 1967. Eventually he became an artist-in-residence at Dartmouth and later was offered a permanent position on the faculty. For decades he lived in Hanover, New Hampshire, during the school year and in the summer returned to Islesford. When he retired in 1995, Islesford became his permanent home. He has lived in France and Germany and has traveled to all parts of the world—always in search of a story. He brings those stories home to Islesford and then shapes them and retells them and illustrates them and sends them along to readers. His interests revolve around art and storytelling, making puppets, and collecting myriad toys. His interests do not extend to cooking. He says, "I'm no hand at cooking." But he extols the cooking ability of his sister Elaine. "She," says Bryan, "would answer any questions you might wish to know."

Antigua

Ashley Bryan's parents immigrated to the United States from Antigua, a small island in the Caribbean and settled in the Bronx (New York). Antigua was inhabited for centuries before Christopher Columbus sailed from Europe. Columbus sighted the island in passing and named it after Santa Maria la Antigua, the miracle-working saint of Seville. Europeans did not settle the island, though, for nearly a century. The island eventually became the "Gateway to the Caribbean" and a thriving sugar-producing community. Slaves provided most of the labor for the sugar plantations. In 1834, during the reign of King William IV, the British abolished slavery in the empire. Antigua instituted full emancipation and became the earliest to abolish slavery in the British Caribbean. The abolishment of slavery is one milestone that is celebrated during Antigua's annual Carnival festivities.

Bread Pudding

Ashley Bryan's sister, Elaine Martindale, sent along this comment and recipe for one of Ashley's favorite dishes.

"In our house mama did not waste anything. Because some of us would not eat the ends of the bread, she would save them until they got hard and she had enough to make bread pudding. Mama was a great cook, and she never measured anything." Here is the recipe.

Crumble one loaf of hard bread in a bowl. Pour 1 quart of milk over the bread and mash it up. Let mixture soak for one hour or more. Bread will absorb the milk. If it is too dry you can add more milk (it should be mushy). Add 1 cup sugar, 3/4 cup raisins, 1 teaspoon nutmeg, 1 teaspoon cinnamon, 1 1/2 teaspoons vanilla, and 2 beaten eggs. Beat all together with electric mixer. Pour into a buttered 9 x 12 pan. Sprinkle top with cinnamon. Bake in a 350° F oven 45 minutes to 1 hour until a knife inserted into the pudding comes out almost clean. Fruit can be added to mixture if desired—peaches, pears, pineapple, and so on.

Signature Recipe—Elaine Martindale

About Sweet Potatoes

Sweet potatoes are tuberous root vegetables belonging to the same family of plants as the morning glory. The sweet potato is native to Central America and has been cultivated in the southern states since the sixteenth century.

"Our parents came to New York from Antigua, West Indies, after the First World War. Mama was a great cook and she had a lot of mouths to feed. As a child I was always in the kitchen watching and helping mama make 'something out of nothing.' Ashley had no time or interest in cooking. He was too busy drawing and writing."

—Elaine Martindale

Author Ashley Bryan (right)
with his sister, Elaine Martindale.

Sweet Potato Pie

Bake three medium-sized sweet potatoes until tender when pieced with a fork. Peel and mash potatoes while still warm.

Add:

- 1/2 stick butter to warm potatoes
- 1 cup white sugar
- 1/2 cup brown sugar
- 1 teaspoon nutmeg
- 1 teaspoon cinnamon
- pinch of salt
- 1 1/2 teaspoons vanilla
- 1 teaspoon lemon juice
- 1/3 cup canned milk, and
- 3 well-beaten eggs

Mix all ingredients with electric mixture until smooth.

While potatoes are baking, you can take two ready-made pie crusts, pierce the bottom with a fork and bake in a 350° F oven until slightly brown. Pour potato mixture into partially baked pie shell and bake in a 350° F oven for 1 hour until inserted knife comes out clean.

Signature Recipe—Elaine Martindale

Selected Books Written/Illustrated by Ashley Bryan

Ashley Bryan's ABC of African American Poetry. (Atheneum, 1998)

Ashley Bryan's African Tales Un-Huh. (Atheneum, 1998)

Beautiful Blackbird. (Atheneum, 2005)

A Nest Full of Stars: Poems. Text by James Berry. (Greenwillow Books, 2004)

Spirituals. (Atheneum, 2005)

Turtle Knows Your Name. (Atheneum, 1989)

More Tales from the Caribbean

Comissiong, Lynette. *Zebo Nooloo Chinoo.* Illustrated by Rachel Parker. (Macmillan Caribbean, 2003)

MacDonald, Amy. *Please, Malese!: A Trickster Tale from Haiti.* Illustrated by Emily Lasker Hallensleben. (Farrar Straus & Giroux, 2002)

San Souci, Robert D. *Cendrillon: A Caribbean Cinderella.* Illustrated by Brian Pinkney. (Simon & Schuster, 2001)

San Souci, Robert D. *Twins and the Bird of Darkness: A Hero Tale from the Caribbean.* Illustrated by Terry Widener. (Simon & Schuster, 2002)

Eve Bunting—Birthday Cake

Dad and Mom and I take the bus to Battery Park. We're carrying the stuff for the birthday picnic. Mom has the cake. It's October 28, bright and sharp and cold.

—from *A Picnic in October*
by Eve Bunting

Eve Bunting

Birthday: December 19

Favorite place: Laguna Beach and Portrush, Ireland

Favorite foods: Mexican anything

Family:

    Husband—Edward

    Sons—Sloan and Glenn

    Daughter—Christine

    Five grandchildren

Home:

    Childhood—Maghera, Ireland

    Now—Pasadena, California

Eve Bunting is a native of Ireland, having been born in Maghera, Ireland. After marrying Edward Bunting they moved to Scotland, and in 1958, the couple and their three children left Scotland to settle in California. She became a naturalized citizen in 1967. Her children were teenagers when she began to think about writing. She was forty-three years old when her first book, *The Two Giants,* was published by Ginn in 1972. That Irish folktale launched her career—a career that now includes books with myriad themes and topics. Bunting still begins her writing in longhand and always has a pencil and paper close by.

A Picnic in October

An Italian American family takes a picnic lunch and a cake on their annual trip to Liberty Island to celebrate the October birthday of the Statue of Liberty. Mike, the young boy in the family, thinks the trip is not necessary and rather boring. His attitude changes once he observes a family that is new to America, also paying their respects to the symbol of welcoming and freedom.

PATRIOTIC CELEBRATIONS

Celebrate the Statue of Liberty's birthday (dedicated October 28, 1886), honor native-born and naturalized foreign-born citizens on the day of the signing of the Constitution, in 1787—Citizenship Day (September 17), Fourth of July, Flag Day (June 14), on a day an individual becomes a citizen, or any other patriotic holiday with these festive cupcakes.

Surprise Celebration Cupcakes

- 2 chocolate cake mixes
- 2 sticks margarine or butter
- 6 eggs
- 2 cups water

Mix ingredients together. Fill cupcake liners or tins half full. Bake at 350° F for 20 minutes. After the cupcakes are baked, and almost cool, insert the filling by using a large pastry tip or decorator tube.

Filling:

- 1 cup evaporated milk
- 1 cup sugar
- 1 1/3 cups Crisco (do not substitute)
- 1 teaspoon vanilla

Beat with a mixer on high for a minimum of 10 minutes.

Add 1 tablespoon cold water and 1 tablespoon powdered sugar.

Fill a pastry tube for this filling and insert in the center of each cupcake. For holidays the filling might be tinted for the holiday season. Frost each cupcake, covering the hole where the filling was inserted.

Frosting:

Melt over low heat:

- 1/2 cup butter
- 3 squares unsweetened baking chocolate
- 3 squares semisweet chocolate
- Cool butter and chocolate mixture (about 5 minutes) while you combine
- 5 cups confectioner's sugar
- 1 cup sour cream
- 2 teaspoons vanilla extract
- To the sugar mixture add the chocolate and butter ingredients and beat until smooth.

Decorate:

Swirl the frosting on each cupcake, sprinkle with red, white, and blue sprinkles, and put a miniature flag in each cupcake.

The Statue's Birthday

Each year since 1937 (except for 2001) the Ladies Auxiliary to the Veterans of Foreign Wars of the United States has commemorated the original dedication of the Statue of Liberty in 1886 with a special ceremony. The organization regularly donates funds for special projects in relation to the statue. Important people in the history of the statue include: Emma Lazarus, whose poem was placed on a bronze plaque on the pedestal of the statue (1903); Frederic-Auguste Bartholdi, the sculptor who made the statue and who chose Bedloe Island as the statue's home; Eduoard deLaboulaye, the man who conceived the idea of giving a gift to the United States on its hundredth birthday; Roger Morris Hunt, who designed the pedestal for the statue; Charles P. Stone, chief engineer for the construction of the statue's pedestal and concrete foundation; and Joseph Pulitzer, who created a fund-raising plan (publishing names of donors) that raised the final dollars for erecting the statue on its pedestal.

Neapolitan Birthday Cake

This cake will need two cake mixes (one white and one chocolate).

Prepare the cake mixes according to the directions. Plan to bake all layers in pans of equal size. One chocolate layer will not be used for this cake; freeze for later. Add 1 teaspoon of strawberry flavoring or almond flavoring and then use red food paste to color half of the white cake mix to make a strawberry layer.

When layers have been baked, cool on a rack, and if there are any rises on the tops of the layers, use a long knife to even them out.

Let the layers rest while you prepare the Festival Frosting.

Festival Frosting

- 4 egg whites
- 3 cups sugar
- 1/4 teaspoon salt
- 2/3 cup water
- 4 teaspoons light corn syrup
- 2 teaspoons vanilla extract

Combine all ingredients except vanilla in the top of a double boiler over boiling water. Beat with electric mixer for about 7 minutes, or until mixture will stand in stiff peaks. Beat in 2 teaspoons vanilla extract.

Place the layers, chocolate first, strawberry next, and vanilla on top. Between each layer place a generous layer of frosting. Frost the top and sides. Sprinkle red, white, blue confetti sprinkles on to decorate. Add sparklers for a festive patriotic birthday cake.

Selected Books Written by Eve Bunting

Anna's Table. Illustrated by Taia Morley. (NorthWord Press, 2003)

The Bones of Fred Mcfee. Illustrated by Kurt Cyrus. (Harcourt, 2002)

Dreaming of America: An Ellis Island Story. Illustrated by Ben Stahl. (Bridge Water, 1999)

Ducky. Illustrated by David Wisniewski. (Clarion, 1997)

My Special Day at Third Street School. Illustrated by Suzanne Bloom. (Boyds Mills Press, 2004)

A Picnic in October. Illustrated by Nancy Carpentar. (Harcourt, 1999)

Smoky Night. Illustrated by David Diaz. (Harcourt, 1994)

So Far from the Sea. Illustrated by Chris Soentpiet. (Clarion, 1998)

Train to Somewhere. Illustrated by Ronald Himler. (Clarion, 1996)

Coming to America

Bial, Raymond. *Tenement: Immigrant Life on the Lower East Side*. (Houghton, 2002)

Sandler, Martin W. *Island of Hope: The Story of Ellis Island and the Journey to America*. (Scholastic, 2004)

Hoobler, Dorothy, and Thomas Hoobler. *We Are Americans: Voices of the Immigrant Experience*. (Scholastic, 2003)

Maestro, Betsy. *Coming to America: The Story of Immigration*. Illustrated by Susannah Ryan (Scholastic, 1996)

The History of the Statue of Liberty

Hochain, Serge. *Building Liberty: A Statue Is Born*. Illustrated by Camilla Bozzoli. (National Geographic, 2004)

Maestro, Betsy. *The Story of the Statue of Liberty*. Illustrated by Giulio Maestro. (HarperCollins, 1986)

Penner, Lucille Rech. *The Statue of Liberty* (Step-into-Reading, Step 2). (Random House, 1995)

Dori Hillestad Butler—Lefse

I do make lefse every Christmas ... [My Grandmother's recipe is] an unusual recipe in that it doesn't have potatoes in it! ... I remember making it with her. Every time I make lefse, I hear my grandma's voice in my head telling me, "That's not thin enough!"

—Dori Hillestad Butler

Dori Hillestad Butler is a native Minnesotan. She has memories of making lefse with her paternal grandmother. "My grandmother's lefse recipe doesn't have potatoes in it! My husband keeps trying to get me to make what he considers "real" lefse (with potatoes), and I do have another family recipe that has potatoes in it. But it's not my grandma's recipe, it was her nephew's [Tom's] recipe." Dori's grandmother's parents immigrated to the United States from the Hardanger area in Norway. Her grandfather's family came from a small village in Norway called Hillestad hence her birth name, Hillestad.

Butler grew up in southern Minnesota, the town of Fairmont. Each of her parents grew up as an only child, so Butler does not have any aunts, uncles, or cousins. She did not have any siblings until her brother was born when she was eight. She spent a lot of time by herself, reading and writing. Many of her stories were about families with a dozen or more children. Because she did not think she could make a living by writing, she went to college and got degrees in English and child psychology and then went on to graduate school. By that time she was married and her husband encouraged her to take a year off to write—she has been writing ever since. She wrote magazine articles and did some ghost writing for a series. Then, after almost seven years, her first picture book, *The Great Tooth Fairy Rip-Off*, was published. Now she has published several picture books and a couple of novels for young readers.

Dori Hillestad Butler grew up in Minnesota, and when she wrote *M Is for Minnesota* she included information about the state grain, wild rice. "Wild rice," Butler says, "is an aquatic grass that grows along the edges of rivers and in large shallow lakes called rice beds. Wild rice is an important food for the Ojibwe people and also has spiritual meaning for them. To harvest wild rice the traditional way, one person pushes a canoe through the water with a long, forked pole while another person uses a pair of long narrow sticks called rice knockers to pull the rice plant over and beat the ripe kernels into the bottom of the canoe. Today wild rice is also grown commercially in rice paddies." Butler usually makes wild rice soup the day after Thanksgiving and the day after Christmas, using leftover rice and broth made from the turkey carcass.

Wild Rice Soup

Recipe

- 4 tablespoons butter or margarine
- 1/4 cup chopped onion
- 1/4 cup chopped celery
- 1/3 cup flour
- 4 cups chicken or turkey broth
- 2 cups cooked wild rice
- 1 cup cooked chicken or turkey meat
- 1 teaspoon salt
- 1 cup light cream or half and half
- 2 tablespoons dry sherry
- Toasted almonds
- Fresh parsley

Melt butter in saucepan. Sauté onion and celery until tender. Stir in flour and let it bubble. Gradually add broth, stirring constantly. Cook until mixture comes to a boil. Boil 1 minute. Add rice, meat, and salt. Turn heat down and simmer for 5 minutes. Add half and half and sherry. Pour into bowls and sprinkle toasted almonds and fresh parsley on top of each serving.

Signature Recipe—Dori Hillestad Butler

Lefse

Dori Hillestad Butler's grandmother's lefse recipe is made without potatoes. In Norway, lefse without potatoes are called Hardangerlefse. However, the variety of lefse made with potatoes is called "potekaker"—potato cakes. The term "lefse" is used for each variation.

Dori's Grandmother's Lefse (Hardangerlefse)

- 4 1/2 cups sifted flour
- 3 cups milk
- 3/4 cup lard
- 1 tablespoon salt
- 2 teaspoons sugar

Let milk and lard come to a boil, then stir liquid into flour. Shape into 20 balls. Roll thin. Bake on lefse grill at very high heat. Turn over and bake on the other side. Stack and cool on clean cloth towel. Makes 20 lefse (or can cut into 40 pieces).

Tom's Potato Lefse (Potekaker)

- 3 cups mashed potatoes
- 1/2 teaspoon baking powder
- 1 tablespoon sugar
- 1 teaspoon salt
- 3/4 cup sour cream
- 1 1/2 cups flour

Mix mashed potatoes, baking powder, sugar, salt, and sour cream. Cool before adding flour. Roll thin. Bake on lefse grill at high heat. Turn over.

Signature Recipe—Dori Hillestad Butler

Selected Books Written by Dori Hillestad Butler

ABCs of Wisconsin. Illustrated by Alison Relyea. (Trails Books, 2000)

The Great Tooth Fairy Rip-Off. Illustrated by Jack Lindstrom. (Fairview Press, 1997)

H Is for Hoosier: An Indiana Alphabet. Illustrated by Eileen Potts Dawson. (Trails Books, 2001)

M Is for Minnesota. Illustrated by Janice Lee Porter. (University of Minnesota Press, 1998)

My Mom's Having a Baby! Illustrated by Carol Thompson. (Whitman, 2005)

Sliding into Home. (Peachtree, 2003)

Trading Places with Tank Talbott. (Whitman, 2003)

W Is for Wisconsin. Illustrated by Eileen Dawson. (Wisconsin Tales & Trails, 1998)

Books about Rice

Rice is an important crop the world over. It is so important in Japan that two brands of cars were named after rice. Toyota means "bountiful rice field" and Honda means "the main rice field."

Demi. *One Grain of Rice: A Mathematical Folklore.* (Scholastic, 1997)

Dooley, Norah. *Everybody Cooks Rice.* (CarolRhoda, 1992)

Rosa-Casanova, Sylvia. *Mama Provi and the Pot of Rice.* (Atheneum, 1997)

Sendak, Maurice. *Chicken Soup with Rice.* (HarperCollins, 1962)

Toni Buzzeo—Pumpkin Pie Pizzazz

Photo: Sharron L. McElmeel

When the pumpkins ripened on the vine in sunburnt autumn,
we carried them across the island
and baked pumpkin pies with Mama.

—from *Sea Chest* by Toni Buzzeo

Toni Buzzeo

Birthday: October 4

Favorite place: Library

Favorite foods: Pumpkin pie &
  Italian food

Family:

   Spouse—Ken Cyll

   Son—Christopher "Topher"

Home:

   Childhood—Michigan

   Now—Maine

Toni Buzzeo grew up in Michigan. For the first ten years of her life she was an only child with a special relationship with her Grandma Mae. When Toni finally got a sibling it was a foster sister, a nine-month old who was awaiting adoption. A few months after Marianne left with her adoptive family, Toni became a sister for keeps when her sister Karen was born. Later two brothers, David and Glen joined the family and the Buzzeos moved across town where Toni became acquainted with two brothers, Ken and Mike Cyll who lived next door. Mike became one of her best friends and Ken eventually became her husband. While she was growing up her family told stories, cooked, visited the library, and enjoyed grandparents and family get-togethers. Pumpkin pie was a family favorite.

When Toni and Ken married, they settled in Maine in a historic two-story saltbox on a thirty-five acre farm—the remains of a larger farm. The acres have given them plenty of room to plant a garden. They grow their own pumpkins and in the fall when the leaves are golden on the trees they harvest their crop, carve some and bake others. The fresh pumpkin pulp is used to make some of the most delicious pumpkin pies.

When Toni was writing *Sea Chest* the book emerged as a book about adoption and family relationships, especially the relationship between the sisters. In the book, Toni speaks of Maita being an only child for the first ten years of her life and her experiences when a sister does arrive—in a sea chest washed ashore. She describes the autumn display of oranges and reds and of course, pumpkins. Nothing would represent family closeness and good times more than a day spent baking a pumpkin pie.

Toni writes about her life and work in *Toni Buzzeo and You* (Libraries Unlimited, 2005).

PUMPKIN BLOSSOMS

The pumpkin blossoms on each plant are what eventually become pumpkins. Larger pumpkins are often carved as Jack-o-lanterns. Smaller pumpkins are often baked and the flesh pureed to use in baking pies, cakes, or custard.

Cooking Pumpkin Blossoms

The pumpkin blossoms are dipped in egg, covered with bread crumbs and fried in butter. For one dozen pumpkin blossoms you will need:

- 3 eggs beaten
- 12 saltine crackers
- 1/8 pound (or 1/2 stick) butter or margarine
- salt and pepper

Crush crackers in a shallow bowl, salt and pepper to taste. Beat eggs in a second shallow bowl. Dip blossoms in egg and gently roll in cracker crumbs. Fry in a frying pan until golden brown. Remove from pan. Drain on a paper towel.

Baking the Pumpkins

A small pie pumpkin generally yields approximately four cups of pumpkin for cooking or baking. Preheat over to 400° F. Remove the stem. Cut each pumpkin in two parts. Place face down on a baking sheet and place in the oven. Bake until the outer rind is soft and shiny. Scoop out the pumpkin flesh and mash or blend until it is the consistency of mashed potatoes and not stringy. Measure and use fresh or freeze for use later. If recipe calls for canned pumpkin you may wish to decrease other liquids if using fresh pumpkin.

Pumpkin Pie Pizzazz

Pie Pan Crust

Ingredients:

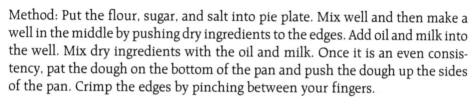

- 1 1/2 cups flour
- 1/4 cup sugar
- 1/2 teaspoon salt
- 1/2 cup oil
- 2 tablespoons milk

Method: Put the flour, sugar, and salt into pie plate. Mix well and then make a well in the middle by pushing dry ingredients to the edges. Add oil and milk into the well. Mix dry ingredients with the oil and milk. Once it is an even consistency, pat the dough on the bottom of the pan and push the dough up the sides of the pan. Crimp the edges by pinching between your fingers.

Pumpkin Pie Filling

Combine the following ingredients with 1 1/2 cups of fresh mashed pumpkin (or canned pumpkin if you are unable to obtain the fresh):

- 3/4 cup sugar
- 3 slightly beaten eggs
- 1 cup milk
- 6-ounce can evaporated milk
- 1/2 teaspoon salt
- 1 teaspoon cinnamon
- 1/2 teaspoon cloves
- 1/2 teaspoon ginger
- 1/2 teaspoon nutmeg

Pour into unbaked pie crust (crimp edges high). Bake in a 400° F oven for approximately 50 minutes or until a knife, inserted in the center, comes out clean. Cool and serve with whipped cream or half walnut garnish.

Selected Books Written by Toni Buzzeo

Dawdle Duckling. Illustrated by Margaret Spengler. (Dial Books for Young Readers, 2003)

Little Loon and Papa. Illustrated by Margaret Spengler. (Dial Books for Young Readers, 2004)

Ready or Not, Dawdle Duckling. Illustrated by Margaret Spengler. (Dial Books for Young Readers, 2005)

Sea Chest. Illustrated by Mary Granpré. (Dial Books for Young Readers, 2002)

Pumpkin Books

From Seed to Pumpkin by Jan Kottke. (Children's Book Press, 2000)

Picking Apples & Pumpkins by Amy Hutchings and Richard Hutchings. (Cartwheel Books, 1994)

Pumpkin, Pumpkin by Jeanne Titherington. (William Morrow, 1986)

The Pumpkin Book by Gail Gibbons. (Holiday House, 1999)

The Pumpkin Patch by Elizabeth King. (Puffin; Reprint edition 1996)

Too Many Pumpkins by Linda White, illustrated by Megan Lloyd. (Holiday House, 1997)

Pumpkins by Rynn Williams. (Metro Books, 2000)

Janie Bynum—Banana Bread

Altoona Baboona flicks peas with a spoon-a …

—from *Altoona Baboona*
by Janie Bynum

Janie Bynum

Birthday: March 2

Favorite place: Southwest France and the Bahamas (so far)

Favorite foods: almost any kind of seafood—especially crab; dark chocolate and almost all nuts (especially together)

Family:
Son—Taylor Kromdyk

Home:
Childhood—Dallas and nearby east Texas

Now—Wimberley, Texas, just southwest of Austin

Janie Bynum spent her first twenty-three years in Texas where she grew up with an older sister and brother and later attended the University of North Texas. She then found herself living in the Midwest, working as a graphic designer, attending the School of the Art Institute of Chicago (SAIC). In 1996, as a class assignment at SAIC, she developed a book dummy. That dummy became *Altoona Baboona* and set Janie off on a course that took her into the world of children's books. That first book showcased many things that are important to her: An illustration in *Altoona Baboona* uses the refrigerator to show items that have a connection to things that are important to her. The book's dedication page shows a "snapshot" of a monkey family that represents her parents, Jack and Bea Bynum, her Dallas nephews, Logan and Baron Farmar, riding in a wheelbarrow being pushed by her son, Taylor. In 2004, Bynum packed up her belongings—including the Macintosh computer that she uses to create her digital pen-and-ink and watercolor illustrations, and moved back to Texas.

Illustration: © 1999, Janie Bynum from Altoona Baboona (Harcourt).

"You see, Altoona and I were never fond of canned peas. If you notice in the accompanying art she has coupons for peas on the fridge. Why, you ask, would she buy peas if she hates them? Because she likes to flick them into the sink when she is bored! And, Altoona is very bored on her dune-a—with no friends to share her famous nut bread! (Note the banana nut bread on the counter, bananas on the top of the refrigerator.) Altoona and I both love to cook and eat yummy foods. We love to travel the world, tasting delicious morsels from every culture we encounter. But what we love most is sharing that good food with friends and family."

—Janie Bynum

Banana Bake

Make a graham cracker crumb crust using the following ingredients:
- 1 1/4 cups graham cracker crumbs
- 1/4 cup sugar
- 1/4 cup butter

Mix thoroughly and pat into a greased 8-inch square baking pan. Bake 5 to 6 minutes at 375 degrees or until browned. While crust is baking, begin to prepare topping. In a sauce pan (low heat), melt and combine the following:
- 1/4 cup butter
- 1 teaspoon dried lemon peel
- 1 tablespoon lemon juice

Add 4 firm bananas, cut in 1/2-inch slices, to the butter mixture and turn banana slices over until slices are coated with butter. Put banana slices on the crust; and sprinkle with:
- 1/4 cup brown sugar, firmly packed
- nutmeg, to taste

Bake at 375° F for 12 to 15 minutes or until bubbly. Cut into squares while still warm and serve. Cut into 8 squares.

Variation: Before adding the 1/4 cup brown sugar, sprinkle bananas with 1/2 cup chocolate chips or butterscotch chips; add 1/4 cups chopped nuts.

Banan-O Choc-O Pops and Nutty Spots

Recipe

Pops

Peel 3 bananas; make sure all stringy fibers are removed. Cut in half widthwise. Put an ice cream stick in the cut end of each half. Place on a cookie sheet and cover with plastic wrap. Freeze; this will take about 3 hours in the freezer.

In the microwave, melt 2 to 6 chocolate bars (about 3 to 9 ounces total) on high for about 2 minutes or until chocolate is melted. Dip the bananas in the chocolate, coating as much as possible. (You can use more chocolate to allow for dipping and then make "spots"—see below).

(Optional: Roll chocolate covered bananas in coconut or crushed nuts.) Put bananas on a piece of waxed paper (on a cooking sheet or plate) and return the pops to the freezer until ready to serve.

Spots

Using the leftover chocolate, mix in dried fruit or nuts of any type—drop by spoonfuls onto a cookie sheet and put into the freezer to harden.

Altoona Baboona's Banana Nut Bread

- 1/2 cup butter (softened), plus a little bit to grease the pan
- 1 cup plus 1 tablespoon sugar
- 1 teaspoon baking soda
- 2 eggs
- 1/2 cups pecans, chopped
- 1 teaspoon vanilla
- 1/2 teaspoon salt
- 3 ripe bananas, mashed
- 2 cups flour

Lightly butter and flour one regular-sized metal loaf pan (approximately 9 x 5 inches at the top).

Peel and mash bananas in a shallow bowl. Set aside.

With a mixer, cream butter, sugar, eggs, and vanilla in a large mixing bowl. Sift together flour, soda and salt in another bowl. Using a wooden spoon or spatula, add to dry mixture: one-third bananas, then one-third flour mixture. Continue until bananas and flour mixture are used up. Add nuts and stir well.

Pour into prepared loaf pan and bake at 350° F for 1 hour (or more). Test at 1 hour. Knife inserted in top will come out clean. Do not overbake or bread will be dry.

Signature Recipe—Janie Bynum

Selected Books Written/Illustrated by Janie Bynum

Altoona Baboona. (Harcourt, 1999)

Altoona Up North. (Harcourt, 2001)

Bathtime Blues. Text by Kate McMullan. (Little Brown, 2005)

Edna, the Elephant. Text by Margaret Park Bridges. (Candlewick Press, 2002)

Hokey Pokey. Text by Lisa Wheeler. (Little Brown, 2005)

Naptime for Slippers. Text by Andrew Clements. (Dutton, 2005)

Otis (Harcourt, 2000)

Porcuping: A Prickly Love Story. Text by Lisa Wheeler. (Megan Tingley, 2003)

Rock-a-Baby Band. Text by Kate McMullan. (Little Brown, 2004)

Slippers at Home. Text by Andrew Clements. (Dutton, 2005)

Too Big, Too Small. Text by Frances Minters. (Harcourt, 2001)

Monkeys and Bananas

Aylesworth, Jim. *Naughty Little Monkeys.* Illustrated by Henry Cole. (Dutton, 2003)

Christelow, Eileen. *Don't Wake Up Mama!* (Clarion, 1993)

Christelow, Eileen. *Five Little Monkeys Jumping on the Bed.* (Clarion, 1989)

Christelow, Eileen. *Five Little Monkeys Sitting in a Tree.* (Clarion, 1991)

Christelow, Eileen. *Five Little Monkeys Wash the Car.* (Clarion, 2000)

Christelow, Eileen. *Five Little Monkeys with Nothing to Do.* (Clarion, 1996)

Sierra, Judy. *Counting Crocodiles.* (Gulliver, 1997)

Eric Carle—German Style Potato Dumplings

Photo:: Sharron L. McElmeel

[If he were not an artist, what would he be?] a chef! … I think it would be fun to wear a white apron and a chef's hat and cook up a delicious meal.

—**Eric Carle**

Eric Carle was born in Syracuse, New York, on June 25, 1929. When he was six years old his parents, who emigrated from Germany, took the family back to Stuttgart, Germany, where Carle grew to adulthood. Four years after returning to Germany, when Carle was just ten years old, his father was taken into the German army. Carle did not see his father again until he was eighteen, when his father returned from a Russian prisoner-of-war camp. Carle's school days were very rigid and did little to stimulate creativity. But he had his memories of the Sunday walks in the German forests with his father, who would tell him about the deer, foxes, rabbits, and owls. For a time Carle wanted to be a forester, but he always returned to what he loved best, drawing pictures. When the war came, children in Stuttgart were sent to small villages outside of the city. The villages were thought to be safer than the cities where bombings occurred regularly. It was in a small village of about a dozen farmers and their families that Carle came to know about the communal milk house. Images of the old man who cut grass each morning for his two cows, the farmer's daughter who guarded the cows, and the thick-walled church in the next village are images that have inspired some of the artwork in his books. The village is also where he learned about making pancakes. All of these experiences contribute to his art and his books.

He returned to the United States when he was twenty-two years old and began his career as an art director. Leo Lionni helped him obtain his first job and became his mentor. Later, Bill Martin, Jr., saw a poster featuring a big red lobster that Carle had created and asked him to illustrate the first edition of *Brown Bear, Brown Bear: What Do You See?* That began Carle's association with picture books and changed his life. Perhaps his best-known book is *The Very Hungry Caterpillar.*

Selected Books Written/Illustrated by Eric Carle

Brown Bear, Brown Bear, What Do You See? Text by Bill Martin, Jr. (Henry Holt, 1992 revised)

My Very First Book of Colors. (Philomel, 2005)

My Very First Book of Shapes. (Philomel, 2005)

Pancakes, Pancakes. (Knopf, 1970)

Panda Bear, Panda Bear, What Do You See? Text by Bill Martin, Jr. (Henry Holt, 2003)

"Slowly, Slowly, Slowly," said the Sloth. (Philomel, 2003)

10 Little Rubber Ducks. (HarperCollins, 2005)

The Very Hungry Caterpillar. (Crowell, 1969; Philomel, 1994)

Walter the Baker. (Knopf, 1972; Simon & Schuster, 1995)

In 1976, just twenty-five years after leaving Germany, Eric Carle was a dinner guest at the Ronneburg Restaurant in Amana, Iowa. Carle's critique of the German style meal: "That was the best food I have had since leaving Germany." Elsie Oehler gathered the best of the Ronneburg's recipes into the *Ronneburg Recipe Album: German Style Cooking*. The Ronneburg's recipe for potato dumplings is an excellent accompaniment to many meat courses.

Potato Dumplings

- 1 pound boiled potatoes, peeled and riced
- 1 1/2 cups finely ground bread crumbs
- 1/4 cup onion, chopped
- 2 tablespoons butter
- 1/2 cup flour
- 3 eggs
- 1/4 cup celery, chopped Topping
- 1/2 cup bread crumbs
- 2 tablespoons butter
- 1 teaspoon salt

Boil, peel, and put potatoes through ricer. Sauté onion and celery in butter until tender. Add to potatoes. Sprinkle with crumbs, flour, and salt. Add 3 eggs and mix well with hands. When thoroughly mixed, dip hands in water and roll into 2-inch balls. To cook, place balls in boiling, salted water and cook until balls float to the surface. Remove with a slotted spoon and transfer to a serving dish. To make topping, sauté butter and crumbs over low heat until golden brown. Due to the variations in potatoes, you may have to adjust amounts for crumbs and flour. Dumplings should be firm and hold their shape well. Makes about 10 dumplings.

Ronnebury Recipe Album: German Style Cooking
by Elsie Oehler (1981)

German Pancakes

Ingredients:

- 6 eggs
- 1 1/4 cups flour
- 1/2 teaspoon salt
- 1 tablespoon sugar
- 2 cups milk
- Butter or shortening for the griddle

Beat the eggs and add milk; beat again. In separate bowl, mix flour, salt, and sugar. Mix wet and dry ingredients together, alternating milk mixture and flour mixture together. Let batter set half an hour.

Use iron pan or griddle on medium heat. Melt butter or shortening in the bottom of the pan or griddle. Use about a 1/4 cup batter per pancake. When bubbles appear and begin to burst on one side, flip the cake to the other side and cook until brown.

More Pancake Books

Along with Carle's *Pancakes, Pancakes* read more books on this tasty subject:

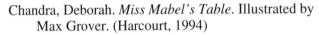

Chandra, Deborah. *Miss Mabel's Table*. Illustrated by Max Grover. (Harcourt, 1994)

dePaola, Tomie. *Pancakes for Breakfast*. (Harcourt, 1978)

Fearnley, Jan. *Mr. Wolf's Pancakes*. (ME Media LLC, 2001)

Many, Paul. *The Great Pancake Escape*. Illustrated by Scott Goto. (Walker, 2002)

McPhail, David M. *Piggy's Pancake Parlor*. (Dutton, 2002)

Nicolai, Margaret. *Kitaq Goes Ice Fishing*. Illustrated by David Rubin. (Alaska Northwest Books, 1998)

Numeroff, Laura Joffe. *If You Give a Pig a Pancake*. (Laura Geringer, 1998)

Pollard, Debbie. *Penelope Penguin's Pancake Party*. (Petland Press, 2000)

Saint James, Synthia. *Sunday*. (Whitman, 1996)

Tate, Carole. *Pancakes & Pies: A Russian Folk Tale*. (Bedrick, 1989)

Wise, William. *Perfect Pancakes If You Please*. Illustrated by Richard Egielski. (Kial, 1997)

Mary Casanova—Crazy Chocolate Cake

Photo: Charles Casanova

This is my overdue tribute to two unassuming, generous women [Dorothy and Ione] who made a difference in my life.

—Mary Casanova
(speaking of her family's
two surrogate grandmothers)

"In my early years as a children's author, I was juggling writing time with being the mother of two young children (Kate was seven and Eric was four when I was working on my first novel, *Moose Tracks*). We had no grandparents living nearby, writing time and money were scarce, but a god-sent answer came in the form of two elderly local women, Dorothy and Ione. During those early family years, they each adopted our family—and we adopted them as surrogate grandmothers. Between their frequent visits, these two women passed on their love of knitting, cards, cooking, and game playing. . . . My kids benefited from our relationships with "Grandma Dorothy" and "Grandma Ione" (I now think of them as saints!), and I found a few extra hours to turn to my computer and write.

[The recipe for Crazy Eggless Chocolate Cake] is a recipe these women both loved and shared with me. Dorothy and Ione have both passed on, but whenever I bake this cake I think of them. Though writing is hard work, many hands and hearts have helped me along the way. This is my overdue tribute to two unassuming, generous women who made a difference in my life."

—Mary Casanova

Mary Casanova

Mary Casanova's love of the out-of-doors is evident in all of the books she writes. As a child, the power of words had difficulty competing with her love of horseback riding, skiing, swimming, and all the other active things that she wanted to do. Her brother and sisters (ten in all) often played tag off the family pontoon boat. In the winter, they all played ice hockey. But in high school, she "fell in love with the power and magic of words." She has been writing ever since. After marrying Charles Casanova, the couple, acting on their joint love of nature, moved to northern Minnesota, on the Canadian border. Their barn-style house, built at the turn-of-the-century, provides a view of many of nature's animals and of the bridge that leads into Canada. In 2004, Casanova got her own horse, Lexi. The horse is a nine-year-old Morgan mare, and Mary says, "There's nothing quite like owning a horse." Don't be surprised if Lexi shows up in one of Mary's adventure books.

Collaborative Books: Read and Compare with *One Dog Canoe*

Allen, Pamela. *Who Sank the Boat?* (Putnam, 1983)

Bratney, Sam. *Guess How Much I Love You.* Illustrated by Anita Jeram. (Candlewick Press, 1995)

Brett, Jan. *The Mitten* (Putnam, 1989)

Burningham, John. *Mr. Grumpy's Outing.* (Henry Holt, 1995)

Numeroff, Laura Joffe. *If You Give a Mouse a Cookie.* Illustrated by Felicia Bond. (HarperCollins, 1985)

Tresselt, Alvin. *The Mitten.* (HarperTrophy, 1989; pb)

COCOA POWDER

There are two types of unsweetened cocoa powder: natural and Dutch-processed. It is best to use the type specified in the recipe because the leavening agent used is dependent on the type of cocoa powder. Some prefer using Dutch-processed cocoa because a slight bitterness may be tasted in cakes using natural cocoa and baking soda. When natural cocoa (an acid) is used in recipes calling for baking soda (an alkali), it creates a leavening action that causes the batter to rise when placed in the oven.

Double Dutch—
Chocolate Cherry Nut Cookies

Cream until light and fluffy:

- 1 cup unsalted butter, room temperature
- 1 cup light brown sugar
- 1/2 cup white granulated sugar

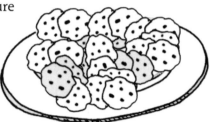

Add and beat until mixed in:

- 2 large eggs
- 2 teaspoons pure vanilla extract

Sift together these ingredients, add to butter mixture:

- 2 cups all-purpose flour
- 1/2 cup Dutch-processed cocoa powder
- 1 teaspoon baking soda
- 1/4 teaspoon salt

Fold in:

- 2 cups chocolate chips/bits
- 1 cup dried cherries, cut in chunks
- 1 cup walnut pieces (or substitute pecans)

Form dough into 1-inch balls and place on a baking sheet about 2 inches apart.

Cookies should be baked, on the center rack of a preheated 350° F oven, until they are soft in the center and firm around the edges—about 8 minutes. Remove from oven—let cookies cool about 5 minutes. Completely cool the cookies. Makes about eighty 2-inch cookies.

Crazy Eggless Chocolate Cake

Preheat oven to 350° F.

Grease and flour 2 round cake pans or 1 9 x 13 pan.

In a medium bowl, combine and stir:

- 3 cups unbleached flour
- 2 teaspoons soda
- 1 teaspoon salt
- 2 cups white sugar
- 1/2 cup cocoa powder

In a small bowl, combine:

- 3/4 cup vegetable oil
- 1 teaspoon vanilla
- 2 teaspoons vinegar
- 2 cups lukewarm water

Add liquid ingredients to dry. Stir until blended, but do not beat. Pour into pans and bake for approximately 30 minutes (or until toothpick comes out clean when tested in center).

Cool for 10 minutes on rack. Turn over onto racks after a few minutes. Cool completely.

Frosting:

Bring to boil and boil for 1 minute:

- 1 cup sugar
- 1/3 cup cocoa powder
- 1/3 cup milk

Add:

- 1/3 cup butter
- 1/3 cup peanut butter
- 1 teaspoon vanilla

Cool, frost, and enjoy.

Signature Recipe—Mary Casanova

Selected Books Written by Mary Casanova

Cécile: Gates of Gold. (Pleasant, 2002)

Curse of a Winter Moon. (Hyperion, 2000)

The Hunter. Illustrated by Ed Young. (Atheneum, 2000)

Moose Tracks. (Hyperion, 1995)

One-Dog Canoe. Illustrated by Ard Hoyt. (Farrar, Straus & Giroux, 2003)

When Eagles Fall. (Hyperion, 2002)

Judith Caseley—Broccoli, Cookies, and More

Mama gives us all a snack.
Melissa says, "Cookie!" and eats one up.
Then she points to Lucy and says, "Friend!"
Cookie, Friend. Two nice new words. I eat my cookie also.

—from *Sisters* by Judith Caseley

Judith Caseley

Birthday: October 17

Favorite foods: pizza, coffee, cookies, ice cream, salad

Family: two sisters and a brother

    Daughter—Jenna

    Son—Michael

Home:

    Childhood—New Jersey

    Now—New York (Long Island)

"Pizza has always been an all-time favorite, and is featured in my book, *On the Town: A Community Adventure.* A young boy explores his community and eats dinner with his family at the pizza parlor. I took pictures of my local restaurant, painting its bright Italian tiles. In *Sisters,* a book about a little girl and her adopted sister, Kika likes eating the pizza crust, as her sister Melissa notes, just like her new mother does. My own mother, Dorothy, a crust eater herself, was very health conscious, and would never serve us pizza without a large salad to go along with it … something green to counteract something you felt guilty eating!"

—Judith Caseley

According to the *Guinness Book of World Records*, the largest pizza ever made was made in South Africa in December 1990 at the Norwood Hypermarket, and measured 123 feet in diameter!

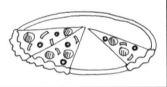

English Muffin Pizza

Most mozzarella you see today is made in the U.S. from cow's milk, but traditionally it was produced from water buffalo milk, which had been cured.

Not the traditional type of pizza one might order from the pizza shop but these pizzas are fun to make with several young hands who want to make their own versions.

Assemble toppings in individual bowls: pepperoni slices, cooked hamburger, shredded cheeses: Mozzarella Cheese, Monterey Jack Cheese, Cheddar Cheese; onions, olives—whatever your guests might want to put on a pizza.

Place English muffin halves on a cookie sheet. Spread each half with pizza sauce (the new squirt bottles work well for young pizza makers). Each person creates their own pizza by placing toppings on their own muffins. If several are making pizzas—you will want to make a design of sorts on top of each muffin to help distinguish which pizza is which. For example: sliced olives, tomatoes, or peppers could be used to make an initial on the top of each pizza.

Top with shredded cheese. Place in a 350° F oven for approximately 15 minutes. Serve hot.

Pizza Books

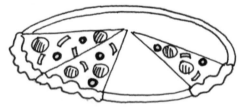

Dobson, Christina. *Pizza Counting*. Illustrated by Matthew Holmes. (Charlesbridge, 2003)

Gelman, Rita Golden. *Pizza Pat* (Step-Into-Reading, Step 2). (Random House, 1999)

Holub, Joan. *The Pizza That We Made*. Illustrated by Lynne Cravath. (Viking, 2001)

Pelham, David. *Sam's Pizza: Your Pizza to Go*. (Dutton, 1996)

Steig, William. *Pete's a Pizza*. (HarperCollins, 1998)

Sturges, Philemon. *The Little Red Hen Makes a Pizza*. Illustrated by Amy Walrod. (Dutton, 1991)

Judith Caseley

Judith Caseley grew up in a home in New Jersey and then enrolled in Syracuse University where she earned a degree in fine arts in 1973. At first she painted for exhibit in various galleries and private collections. Eventually she turned to writing and illustrating children's books and found that very satisfying. She draws on her own life's experiences to write her books—her stage fright, her relationship with her grandfather, stories from her Russian ancestors—many told by her Grandmother Rebecca, and her love for food. Her characters eat popcorn, spaghetti, French toast, muffins, pizza, and cookies and ice cream.

Origin of *Rocco's Broccoli So That You Can Eat Ice Cream Later*

"After the death of both parents and my own divorce, all in the same year, I started tap dancing at a local dance school. After the class, my new friends and I would go to the Italian men's club next door to drink cappuccino while the men played cards. It meant one sleepless night a week, as Rocco refused to make decaffeinated coffee, but the club became my home away from home for a year. On Sunday afternoons, Rocco would make my favorite healthy dish, broccoli rabe, never featured in a book, but something green and delicious that I would eat with a hunk of bread so I could consume a dish of ice cream later, guilt-free!"

—**Judith Caseley**

Rocco's Broccoli So That You Can Eat Ice Cream Later

Partially steam a bunch of broccoli rabe in a steamer.

Heat up some olive oil in a large pan, with several cloves of diced garlic, until cooked.

Throw broccoli rabe in the pan, reduce heat to a low light, and cook 10 to 15 more minutes.

Add balsalmic vinegar and olive oil and toss. Salt and pepper to taste.

Eat hot or cold with Italian bread.

Signature Recipe—Judith Caseley

Selected Books Written/Illustrated by Judith Caseley

Bully. (Greenwillow, 2001)

Dear Annie. (Greenwillow, 1991)

Field Day Friday. (Greenwillow, 2000)

Mama Coming and Going. (Greenwillow, 1994)

On the Town: A Community Adventure. (Greenwillow, 2002)

Sisters. (Greenwillow, 2004)

Sophie and Sammy's Library Sleepover. (Greenwillow, 1993)

Sugar Cookies for Friends

These sugar cookies are easy enough to make that friends of all ages can make and decorate them easily.

Blend together:

- 1/2 cup shortening
- 1/2 teaspoon salt
- 1 teaspoon grated lemon rind
- 1 cup sugar

Beat in:

- 1 egg
- 2 tablespoons milk

Stir in:

- 2 cups flour
- 1 teaspoon baking powder
- 1/2 teaspoon soda

The dough should be well blended. Drop by rounded teaspoons on lightly greased baking sheet. Grease the bottom of a glass. Dip glass in sugar, then use the sugar bottom of the class to flatten the cookie. Sprinkle with nutmeg.

Bake cookies at 350° F for 8 to 10 minutes until cookie is slightly brown, cool on rack. Makes three dozen cookies.

Shirley Climo—Sherbet

Photo: Al Weisberger

Shirley Climo

Birthday: November 25

Favorite place: anyplace by any ocean—any ocean!

Favorite foods: Almost everything (unfortunately); I'm easy to please and enjoy cooking.

Family:

    Spouse—George Climo

    Daughters—Susan and Lisa; and five grandchildren, four granddogs, and eight grandcats.

Home:

    Childhood—Cleveland, Ohio

    Now—Los Altos, California, for the past 50 years

"[The guests] sat on silk cushions and helped themselves to heaping trays of roast lamb and whitefish, to spiced cucumbers, sweet oranges and tart rhubarb, and to goblets of sherbet cooled with mountain snow."

—from *The Persian Cinderella*
by Shirley Climo

In Cleveland, Ohio, the city of her birth, Shirley Climo wrote scripts for a weekly juvenile series, *Fairytale Theatre*. Later, while living in Los Altos, California, she became a writer of children's tales. Once again, she was retelling her own versions of fairy tales. Among her most popular tales are her retellings of Cinderella.

"Around the world, there are more than 800 versions of the Cinderella Story. Each is unique to the place it is told, and one way to emphasize the geographic differences is by introducing regional foods. In my retelling of the Persian Cinderella, Setterah, the heroine, attends a New Year's or No Ruz feast. [The guests ate ... goblets of sherbet....] Sherbet, both the word and the dish, originated in Persia, where it is spelled sherbat in Farsi. For a thousand years, the pulp and juice of fruit, such as apricots, has been sweetened (usually with honey), beaten smooth, and then chilled with the ice from the highest mountain slopes."

—**Shirley Climo**

From his pail he pulled a pasty, a turnover stuffed with meat and potato and made fresh by his good wife, Molly, that morning. Tom was so hungry he swallowed most of it in one great gulp.

—from *Magic and Mischief: Tales from Cornwall* by Shirley Climo

Magic and Mischief is a collection of tales from Cornwall. In that southwest corner of England, a pasty (pronounced with a long "a" sound) is the equivalent of our hot dog or hamburger. Hot from the hearth or cold in a lunch pail, this turnover is the national Cornish dish. It's held by both hands and eaten from side to side, like corn on the cob. That's why the pasty's nickname is "the Cornish mouth-organ." A pastry crust is rolled out and then filled with bits of meat, potatoes, onions, turnips, or whatever else is left in the stew pot. The closest dish on the Western side of the Atlantic Ocean is probably a pot pie.

—Shirley Climo

Cornish Pasty

- 1 potato, cut and diced in 1/4-inch cubes
- 1 medium onion, chopped
- 8 ounces beef, blade or rump
- 1 cup flour
- 1/4 cup butter
- 1/4 cup lard (or solid and cold shortening)
- cold water to mix
- a beaten egg or milk to mix

Preheat oven to 425° F. Cut and dice the potato, onion, and meat in bowl and toss together so parts are well mixed. In a second bowl, cut the butter into the flour until the butter is very fine. Add about 2 tablespoons of cold water and mix to form a firm dough. Turn out onto a floured surface and knead lightly.

Divide the pastry into fourths; roll out each piece to approximately 6 inches in diameter. Trim by cutting around the edge of a small plate.

In each round pastry, place a quarter of the potato and beef filling on the pastry. Brush the edges with water and fold pastry over and seal the edges, making a half circle. Flute the edges with your fingers or the tines of a fork.

Place on a baking sheet. Brush each with a little beaten egg or milk and bake for 40 to 45 minutes until golden brown.

Serve hot or cold.

Apricot Sherbet

- 2 16-ounce cans apricot halves in light syrup drained
- 2 cups sugar
- 1 quart milk
- 1/4 cup lemon juice

Place apricots in container of blender. Process until smooth, scraping down sides. Add remaining ingredients. Freeze in ice cream freezer. Makes 2 quarts.

Selected Books Written by Shirley Climo

The Egyptian Cinderella. Illustrated by Ruth Heller. (Clarion, 1989)

The Irish Cinderlad. Illustrated by Loretta Krupinski. (Clarion, 1996)

The Korean Cinderella. Illustrated by Ruth Heller. (Clarion, 1993)

Magic and Mischief: Tales from Cornwall. Illustrated by Anthony Bacon Venti. (Clarion, 1999)

Monkey Business. Illustrated by Erik Brooks. (Henry Holt, 2005)

The Persian Cinderella. Illustrated by Robert Florczak. (Clarion, 1996)

Tuko and the Birds: A Tale from the Philippines. Illustrated by Francisco X. Mora. (Henry Holt, 2002)

Monkey Business is a collection of myths and fables about monkeys from all over the world. Erik Brooks's illustrations show fourteen species of monkeys.

Questions from "When Is a Monkey Not a Monkey?" in *Monkey Business* by Shirley Climo.

- Where would you eat a *monkey nut?*
- What is *monkey pie*?

Answers:

- You'd eat *monkey nuts* in England. It's slang for peanuts.

In parts of the United States, *monkey pie* is a nickname for coconut cream pie.

Monkey Pie aka Coconut Cream Pie

Crust

- Make one, 9-inch pastry shell (or use a purchased shell)
- 1/3 cup plus 1 tablespoon shortening or 1/3 cup lard
- 1 cup all-purpose flour
- 1/4 teaspoon salt
- 2 to 3 tablespoons cold water

Cut the shortening into the flour, until shortening is in very small pieces (smaller than a pea), add salt, and very cold water, a tablespoon at time until ball can be formed. Roll out on a floured surface into an 11-inch diameter circle. Fold in fourths and gently lay into a pie plate. Unfold and crimp edges with fingers or tines of a fork. Heat oven to 475° F. Prick bottom and side of crust thoroughly with fork. Bake 8 to 10 minutes or until light brown; cool.

Filling:

- 1/4 cup sugar
- Dash salt
- 3 tablespoons cornstarch
- 1 1/2 cup milk
- 2 egg yolks
- 1/2 teaspoon vanilla
- 1 1/2 ounces coconut; plus 1/2 ounce coconut toasted
- 1/2 pint whipping cream

Combine sugar, salt, cornstarch, and milk in saucepan. Cook till thickened. Remove from heat. Add slightly beaten egg yolks to mixture. Cook for 2 minutes. Remove from heat. Add coconut and vanilla. Cool. When the pudding has cooled, whip cream. Add 1/2 of the whipped cream to pudding and mix. Pour in baked crust. Put rest of whipped cream on top of pie, garnish with toasted coconut. Refrigerate till serving time.

Optional "I can make it myself" filling:

Use 2 boxes of vanilla pudding mix. Prepare as directed except reduce the milk used by 1/2 cup for each mix.

Mix with 1 1/2 ounce coconut.

Put filling into baked pie crust.

Use 2 cups Dream Whip or other prepared whipped cream. Place on top of pie filling. Make swirls or dips in whipped cream. Garnish with 1/2 cup of toasted coconut.

Susan Stevens Crummel—Mexican Roll-ups

[Great-Granny's Magnificent Strawberry Shortcake—the recipe in Cook-a-Doodle-Doo!] is a recipe my mom always used for strawberry shortcake when we were growing up. Our dad loved the biscuit-type cake. It is the recipe Rooster, Turtle, Iguana and Pig used in Cook-a-Doodle-Do.

—Susan Stevens Crummel

Susan Stevens Crummel grew up with an older brother, Jack, and a younger sister, Janet. Their father was a naval officer, so the family lived all over the United States, but the family's roots were in Texas. In the 1800s, Susan's great-great grandparents settled near Kerrville, Texas. When it was time to enter college, Susan returned to Texas and earned undergraduate and graduate degrees from Texas Christian University. Susan's first career was in education. She was a math teacher for thirty years in Fort Worth, Texas. In 1997, her younger sister, Janet Stevens, asked Susan to collaborate with her to write *Shoetown*. The book was a success, and Susan and Janet became regular collaborators. Janet Stevens is a renowned illustrator who often illustrates books authored by other writers and sometimes illustrates books she has written. Janet lives in Colorado and Susan in Texas, so they collaborate by phone, e-mail, and fax. Their brother Jack is the "Jack-of-all-Trades" in *And the Dish Ran Away with the Spoon*.

Susan Stevens Crummel

Birthday: March 3

Favorite place: Maui or the family ranch in the hill country of Texas

Favorite foods: anything

Family:

 Spouse—Richard, a high school principal

 Son—Jason, married to Veronica; the parents of Sophia, a granddaughter born April 13, 2004

 Daughters—Christie and Courtney

Home:

 Childhood—All over the United States

 Now—Texas (Has lived in Fort Worth since graduating from college in 1970.)

Jade's Strawberry Shortcake

Susan Stevens Crummel's mother had a special strawberry shortcake recipe that was shared in Susan and Janet's book, *Cook-a-Doodle-Doo!* Jade's Strawberry Shortcake is a similar recipe, with a biscuit-like shortcake.

Rinse and stem 1 quart fresh strawberries. Slice the strawberries, sprinkle with 1/2 cup sugar, and let stand. Preheat oven to 450° F; and grease an 8-inch, round layer-cake pan. In a mixing bowl, combine:

- 2 cups flour
- 2 tablespoons sugar
- 1 tablespoon baking powder
- 1 teaspoon salt

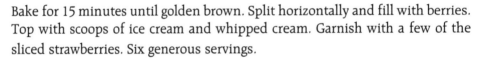

Cut 1/3 cup shortening into the flour mixture, with a pastry blender (or two forks) until crumbly.

Stir in one cup of milk until just blended.

Pat the dough into prepared pan.

Bake for 15 minutes until golden brown. Split horizontally and fill with berries. Top with scoops of ice cream and whipped cream. Garnish with a few of the sliced strawberries. Six generous servings.

Variation: This old-fashioned shortcake or a favorite scone recipe can be used to make strawberry shortcake. Those who enjoy chocolate and strawberries may want to use a chocolate scone or in this recipe substitute 1/3 cup Dutch-processed unsweetened cocoa powder for 1/3 cup of the flour. The resulting biscuit will be a mild chocolate shortcake.

Great-Granny and Little Red Hen

Big Brown Rooster, a main character in *Cook-a-Doodle-Doo!* is the great grandson of "The Little Red Hen." In her story, she generally bakes bread, but when her grandson finds her cookbook, he and the turtle, iguana, and pig discover a delicious shortcake recipe. If you want to become acquainted with Rooster's grandmother, read one of these books.

Downard, Barry. *The Little Red Hen.* (Simon & Schuster, 2004)

Galdone, Paul. *Nursery Classics: A Galdone Treasury.* (Clarion Books, 2001)

Miller, J. P. *The Little Red Hen.* (Golden Books, 2004)

Mexican Roll-ups

Susan lives in Texas and loves to cook Mexican food. She dedicated *Plaidypus Lost* to her bridge group of thirty years. This is the recipe she always serves when they come for dinner.

Chicken Filling:

3 chicken boneless and skinless breasts (precook in 325° oven, covered, until almost done, about 30 minutes. Cut into bite-sized pieces—save the broth!)

In a pan, mix chicken and broth with:

- 2 tablespoons cumin (or more to taste)
- 1 tablespoon chili powder
- 1–2 teaspoons garlic salt

Cook on low heat, stirring occasionally, until mixture cooks down—about an hour. Add water if mixture gets too dry.

Guacamole Topping

- 3 ripe avocados, mashed
- Juice of 1 lemon
- Garlic salt to taste
- 1–2 tablespoons picante sauce

Mix (but not vigorously—it makes it frothy) with fork until blended. Chill.

Pico de Gallo Topping

- 1 small onion, finely chopped
- 3 Roma tomatoes, finely chopped
- 1 fresh jalapeno, finely chopped (optional)
- 1/2 cup cilantro leaves, finely chopped
- Juice of 1 lemon

Mix and chill

To put it all together you will need:

- 12 flour tortillas   • 2 cups grated cheddar cheese   • 8 ounces sour cream

Fill 2 tortillas with chicken filling and roll up. Place on plate, seam side down. Cover with cheese and microwave for 45 seconds (or you can fill all 12 tortillas, top with cheese, put in a baking dish, and heat in oven or microwave). Top with guacamole, then sour cream, then pico de gallo. Serves 6.

Signature Recipe—Susan Crummel

Selected Books Written by Susan Stevens Crummel

And the Dish Ran Away with the Spoon. Illustrated by Janet Stevens. (Harcourt, 2001)

City Dog, Country Dog. Text written with Dorothy Donohue. Illustrated by Dorothy Donohue. (Cavendish Children's Books, 2004)

Cook-a-Doodle-Doo! Illustrated by Janet Stevens. (Harcourt, 1999)

Jackalope. Illustrated by Janet Stevens. (Harcourt, 2003)

Plaidypus Lost. Illustrated by Janet Stevens. (Holiday House, 2004)

Shoetown. Illustrated by Janet Stevens. (Harcourt, 1999)

Tumbleweed Stew. Illustrated by Janet Stevens. (Harcourt, 2000)

Pat Cummings—Chocolate Chip Cookies

Photo: Ai Miki 2002

Baking cookies around Christmas has been a serious undertaking in my family since I can remember. My sisters are much better at it and they use recipes and get great results. The big three are chocolate chips, Christmas bells (a sugar cookie from a recipe my mother got from her mother's cookbook) and oatmeal cookies.

—Pat Cummings

Pat Cummings

Birthday: November 9

Favorite place: her apartment

Favorite foods: all the bad stuff: fish and chips, mac and cheese, dark chocolate, cookies. Some good stuff: fruit, salads, tofu

Family:

   Spouse—Chuku Lee

Home:

   Childhood—Born in Illinois; childhood spent in Virginia, Germany, Kansas, Okinawa

   Now—New York

Pat Cummings grew up with two sisters, Barbara and Linda, and one brother, Artie. Their father was a military man, and the family moved often, but Pat's art helped her to make new friends. Her librarian mother read German fairy tales to the children. Pat says her love of fantasy came from those tales, the fairy-tale castles in Germany and the sense of mysticism and tradition that came from Okinawa, where she lived as a child.

Today, sisters Barbara and Linda are responsible for most of the family cookie baking. Cummings says, "My brother [Artie] and I primarily were *eaters* of cookies, leaving the actual *cooking* to others. I still enter into the Christmas spirit through what I call 'The Cookie Window.' That is—until the cookies bake, until the cookie window opens, there is no holiday." Cummings does sometimes attempt to bake cookies, with interesting results. "The last time … I didn't pay attention to the recipe and used a whole bag of chips, thinking that the recipe on the bag was meant to include all of the chips. So that was a good batch. [The cookies were] *very* chocolaty but apparently not the way to go if you want the cookies in other than liquid form."

A dozen or so years ago, Pat Cummings told an interviewer that her favorite foods were seafood, spinach, cheese, breads, and popcorn. Now, this many years, later she says, "I'm a devotee of all things spinach and, to the extent that I have cooked, my signature dish has been Spinach Surprise. The surprise is that it gets done. I cook in three stages: A day to shop for ingredients. A day or so to mix them up. A day to cook the dish. I don't use a recipe. Not measuring guarantees a surprising result." Her own notes for this dish, a cousin to the spinach quiche, combines both spinach and cheese.

Pat Cummings's Spinach Surprise

- Frozen spinach; quantity depends on appetite
- Cheese, to taste
- Spices, Salt, pepper of course, basil, onion powder (can't tolerate actual onions)
- thyme (occasionally), and nutmeg (a nod to the quiche-connection)
- Mushrooms, as appropriate
- Pine nuts, AHA! one of the occasional surprises
- Brown rice—to separate this from a mere pie or quiche
- Worcestershire Sauce, definitely a splash or three, although sometimes forgotten
- Egg(s), optional to encourage compatibility of ingredients

Mix in a bowl. Pour into a casserole dish. Cook till the cheese melts and it looks "done." Bake in a 300–350° F oven. Although Cummings says, "I have no numbers left on the dial on my stove. I usually set stuff to where I think 300–350° F might once have been."

Signature Recipe—Pat Cummings

Of Pat Cummings's favorite cookies she says, "The chocolate chip recipe is straight Toll House. The oatmeal cookies come from the recipe on the side of the carton. The Christmas Bells recipe is held in trust by my two sisters. It involves mixing dough, dyeing dough, refrigerating dough, cutting dough ... way too many steps. I don't have the recipe, and I don't know if it's a closely guarded secret." Pat (and her brother Artie), the cookie *eaters*, might enjoy an oatmeal cookie with chocolate chips.

Cookie Eater's Oatmeal Chocolate Chip Cookies

Beat the following ingredients until creamy:

- 1 pound (4 sticks) margarine or butter, softened
- 2 cups firmly packed brown sugar
- 1 cup granulated sugar

Add:

- 4 eggs
- 2 teaspoons vanilla

Gradually add the following dry ingredients:

- 3 cups flour
- 2 teaspoons baking soda
- 2 teaspoons ground cinnamon
- 1 teaspoon of salt (optional or lesser amount)
- 6 cups uncooked oatmeal (quick or old fashioned)
- 4 cups (two 12-ounce bags) chocolate chips

Drop dough by rounded tablespoonfuls onto ungreased cookie sheets. Bake in a 350° F oven for 10–12 minutes; or until light golden brown. Cool 1 minute on cookie sheet and then remove to rack to cool completely. Store in tightly covered container. Makes about 8 dozen.

Selected Books Written/Illustrated by Pat Cummings

Ananse and the Lizard: A West African Tale. Written and Illustrated by Pat Cummings. (Henry Holt, 2002)

Angel Baby. Written and Illustrated by Pat Cummings. (HarperCollins, 2000)

The Blue Lake. Written and Illustrated by Pat Cummings. (HarperCollins, 2005)

Clean Your Room, Harvey Moon! Written and Illustrated by Pat Cummings. (Simon & Schuster, 1991)

Just Us Women. Text by Jeannette Franklin Caines. Illustrated by Pat Cummings. (HarperCollins, 1982)

My Aunt Came Back. Written and Illustrated by Pat Cummings. (HarperFestival, 1998; board book)

The World's Wide Open. Text by Bettye Stroud. Illustrated by Pat Cummings. (Simon & Schuster, 2005)

Cookie Books

Adler, David. *Young Cam Jansen and the Missing Cookie* (Viking Easy-to-Read, Level 2). (Viking, 1996)

Blumenthal, Deborah. *The Chocolate-Covered-Cookie Tantrum*. (Clarion, 1999)

Carter, David A. *Who Took the Cookie from the Cookie Jar?: Fun Flaps & Pop-Up Surprises*. (Cartwheel Books, 2002)

Hutchins, Pat. *The Doorbell Rang*. (HarperTrophy, 1989)

Kasza, Keiko. *The Wolf's Chicken Stew*. (Putnam, 1987)

Lass, Bonnie. *Who Took the Cookies from the Cookie Jar?* Illustrated by Philemon Sturges. (Megan Tingley, 2000)

Numeroff, Laura Joffe. *If You Give a Mouse a Cookie*. Illustrated by Felicia Bond. (Laura Geringer, 1985)

Rylant, Cynthia. *The Cookie-Store Cat*. (Scholastic, 2002)

Sabuda, Robert. *Cookie Count: A Tasty Pop-up*. (Little Simon, 1997)

Carl Deuker—Vegetable Medley

Photo: Anne Mitchell

"I won an award for my cooking in the Army," he said, pride in his voice. He tapped himself on the chest. "You didn't know that, did you? Me, Andres Castro. Award-winning chef."

**—Andres Castro
(as quoted by Carl Deuker)**

Carl Deuker

Birthday: August 26

Favorite place: Ballard Locks, Seattle

Favorite foods: salmon, peanut butter, grape nuts, raspberries, cherries, pineapple

Family:

Spouse—Anne Mitchell

Daughter—Marian

Home:

Childhood—Redwood City, California

Now—Seattle, Washington

Carl Deuker was born in San Francisco and grew up in the Bay Area but now lives in Seattle with his family. His father, Jack Deuker, died when he was three, and his older sister Elizabeth was five. His mother, Marie Milligan Deuker, raised the two of them. As an adult Deuker earned a master's degree in English and now teaches fourth- and fifth-grade students in the Northshore School District. He is also a writer of young adult fiction. He carves out an hour or so each day to write, and makes it his goal to write one page a day. In a year's time, he can write 356 pages. He is known for his thrilling sports fiction. Deuker and his teenage daughter, Marian, often attend sports events, and he is teaching her to play golf. She helps him answer his e-mail and sometimes writes information about her dad for his Web site.

Cherry Berry Parfait

Among Carl Deuker's favorite foods are raspberries, cherries, pineapple—this recipe combines those favorites into a very popular parfait dish.

- 1 cup fresh, sweet, dark red cherries
- 1 cup chopped fresh or canned pineapple
- 1 cup fresh raspberries
- 1 cup fresh blueberries
- 1 cup low-fat vanilla or lemon yogurt
- 1 medium sliced banana
- 1/4 cup sliced, toasted almonds

Set aside 4 whole dark red cherries. Remove the pits and slice the remaining cherries in half. In stemmed glasses, layer the cherries, pineapple, raspberries, blueberries, yogurt, and banana. If you wish to make these a day ahead omit the banana because they will likely brown before serving. Sprinkle the almonds on top and garnish with a whole, sweet cherry. Serves four.

ANDRES CASTRO

"When I was in college at Cal Berkeley in the early '70's, I worked food service at the university co-op, a loose collection of housing units. Lunch and dinner were prepared in a central kitchen and then delivered around town. Dinner, served at six, was loaded onto trucks at three, which meant it had to be ready by two. Of course once dinner was in the warmers, it was time to start preparing the next day's lunch. This was hardly an ideal situation for quality. Imagine stuffed bell peppers and rice warming for nearly a full day. Imagine potatoes baked at ten in the morning but not eaten until six in the evening. Imagine salad greens—well, maybe you shouldn't.

"The head chef was Andres Castro, a wonderful man whose mind was as fast as his hands—and I never saw anyone chop an onion faster. Andres was full of tricks to get his student employees to work quickly. He would assign an Arab student to work side-by-side with an Israeli, a Pakistani next to an Indian, an ROTC candidate next to a war protester. The more heated the arguments, the faster the potato peels would fly. Andres would supervise these conversations as well as the food preparation; his sense of humor softened the most strident voices. "Chop! Chop!" he'd call out, his eyes twinkling.

"Faster! Faster!" The basic system made it impossible for the meals to taste good, but Andres did his best every single day, and he made sure the meals went out to the houses on time. Students complained about the food, but no one ever went without.

One late afternoon, when the next day's lunch was safely in the warmers, the next day's dinner salad was in the big refrigerator, and the next day's vegetables were cooking in the oven, Andres told me about his experiences in World War II. He had wanted very much to fight, but some combination of racial prejudice (Andres was Filipino) and health problems had made him a cook. He had been with the troops through many landings in the Pacific, and his stories of the sacrifices made by the men who fought in World War II kept me in the kitchen long after my shift had ended.

"Finally he took his apron off and headed for the door. He'd almost reached it when he turned back. 'I won an award for my cooking in the Army,' he said, pride in his voice. He tapped himself on the chest. 'You didn't know that, did you? Me, Andres Castro. Award-winning chef.'

" 'Really?' I said. 'You won a cooking contest.' I immediately regretted it. The last thing I wanted to do was to hurt his feelings.

"He smiled his impish smile. 'I didn't win for being the best cook, Carl. I won for being the *fastest* cook.' Then the smile went away, and for one of a very few times he was completely serious. 'You may not think that's important, but the soldiers did. You see, they were hungry, and I fed them. And that's what I'm doing for you kids. I'm feeding you. That's been my life.'

"When Andres died, the co-op named one of their dormitories after him, not because he was a great cook, but because he was a great man. He did the best with what he had. I had many great professors at Cal, but no one taught me more than Andres Castro."

— **Carl Deuker**

Chopped Vegetable Salad à la Andres Castro

- 3 or 4 tomatoes, chopped
- 2 cucumbers, chopped
- 1 medium green pepper, chopped
- 1 medium red, orange, or yellow pepper, chopped
- 1 or 2 onions, chopped
- salt and pepper to taste
- 3 tablespoons oil
- 3 tablespoons vinegar
- 1 teaspoon paprika
- 1/2 teaspoon dry mustard
- 1/2 teaspoon, celery seed (optional)

Put all chopped vegetables in a bowl. Mix oil and vinegar. Stir in seasonings and pour over all vegetables. Cover and refrigerate for 12 hours before serving.

Booklist

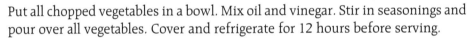

Selected Books Written by Carl Deuker

Night Hoops. (Houghton Mifflin, 2000)

Painting the Black. (Houghton Mifflin, 1997)

Heart of a Champion. (Little, Brown, 1993)

High Heat. (Houghton Mifflin, 2003)

Diane Dillon and Leo Dillon—Plantain Fritters

Big King came.... The servants brought a feast of hog and apples with plantains, fish and coconuts, red beans and rice.

**—from *The Girl Who Spun Gold*
by Virginia Hamilton**

Lionel John Dillon, Jr. (Leo Dillon) and Diane Sorber (Diane Dillon) began life eleven days apart and on opposite coasts. She grew up in the Los Angeles, California, area and he grew up in Brooklyn, New York. Both ended up at Parsons School of Design in 1956 where they met. They married on March 17, 1957. Both were artists, and eventually they began to collaborate and together they combined their efforts to create a third artist—one that, when looking at their own work, even the two of them cannot tell who did what. In 1976 and 1977, they were awarded the most prestigious award in the world of children's books—the Caldecott Award.

Diane says, "Leo's father was a great chef. He brought from the West Indies many delicious recipes that we, as a family, enjoyed. Foods like peme, coo-coo, codfish cakes, and callaloo. He also used unfamiliar vegetables like taro root. Unfortunately, he never wrote the recipes down. Although we helped in the kitchen, we didn't try to write down what he was doing because his measurements were by eye and instinct. Now that he is gone, we regret not trying because now when we attempt to make one of his dishes it never tastes the same."

Diane Dillon and Leo Dillon

Birthdays: Diane, March 13; Leo, March 2

Favorite place: Home

Favorite foods: There is not much that we don't like.

Family:

   Son—Lionel John, III (Lee), also an artist. He is a sculptor and creates jewelry. He has illustrated some books with his parents.

Home:

   Childhood—Diane was born and raised in California; Leo was born in Brooklyn, New York, where he and Diane now live.

> **Coo-coo (or cou-cou):** The Caribbean equivalent of grits. Once based on cassava or manioc meal but now made primarily with cornmeal. Coo-coo is a versatile food that can be baked, fried, or rolled into little balls and poached in soups or stews. Coo-coo is the national dish of Barbados. In Dominica, Antigua, and the Virgin Islands, it is known as "Fungi."

Codfish Cakes

Soak 1 pound fresh codfish in cold water for at least 6 hours (or overnight). Change water at least 3 times during the soaking.

Remove fish from the water and rinse well. Place fish in a saucepan filled with fresh cold water and cook on medium-high heat. Bring the mixture to a simmer and cook for 10 minutes. Drain the fish and let stand until cool enough to handle.

While the fish is cooking mix together in a small bowl and let soak:

- 1/2 cup dried bread crumbs
- 1/2 cup milk

Cook and prepare potatoes to make 2 1/2 cups of mashed potatoes.

After the fish is cooked and cooled, use a fork to flake the fish, remove all bones.

In a large bowl mix the following until well combined:

- Bread crumb/milk mixture
- 2 1/2 cups mashed potatoes
- 2 tbsp melted butter
- 1/2 tsp white pepper
- Dash of hot pepper sauce

Use the fish mixture to form 2 1/2 inch patties or cakes. Heat 1/8 cup of vegetable oil in a large skillet over medium-high heat. Add as many cakes as will fit in one layer in the skillet. Cook until cakes are golden brown on both sides of the cake—about 2 minutes per side.

As cakes are finished cooking, transfer to a warmed platter and cover loosely with foil to keep warm. Repeat the frying process until all cakes are browned.

Serve the cakes warm with a garnish of parsley. (Makes 8–10 cakes.)

Plantain Fritters

Plantains are often eaten in the West Indies and are fairly easy to find in most places now.

Boil and mash 3 ripe plantains

Combine the mashed plantains with:

- 2 tablespoons sugar
- 1/2 teaspoon cinnamon
- 3/4 cup flour (or just enough to make a manageable dough)

Shape the dough into cakes and coat with bread crumbs. Put oil in a skillet and heat. Brown the plantain cakes on both sides in the hot oil. Serve hot.

Selected Books Illustrated by Leo Dillon and Diane Dillon

Ashanti to Zulu: African Traditions. Text by Margaret W. Musgrove. (Dial, 1976)

The Girl Who Spun Gold. Text by Virginia Hamilton. (Blue Sky Press, 2000)

The People Could Fly: American Black Folktales. Text by Virginia Hamilton. (Knopf, 1985)

The Porcelain Cat. Text by Michael P. Hearn. (Little, Brown, 1987; reissue Milk & Honey Press, 2004)

Rap a Tap Tap: Here's Bojangles, Think of That! Text by Leo Dillon and Diane Dillon. (Blue Sky Press, 2002)

Two Little Trains. Text by Margaret Wise Brown. (HarperCollins, 2001)

Where Have You Been? Text by Margaret Wise Brown. (HarperCollins, 2004)

Who's in Rabbit's House? A Masai Tale. Text by Verna Aardema. (Dial, 1977)

Why Mosquitoes Buzz in People's Ears: A West African Tale. Text by Verna Aardema. (Dial, 1975)

Booklist

Spinning the Gold

The Girl Who Spun Gold, by Virginia Hamilton and illustrated by Leo and Diane Dillon, is a West Indian version of the classic German version of the Rumpelstiltskin story. In this story Lit'mahn spins thread into gold cloth for the king's new bride.

Here are some other books with a similar theme.

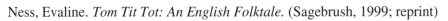

Ness, Evaline. *Tom Tit Tot: An English Folktale*. (Sagebrush, 1999; reprint)

Zelinsky, Paul O. *Rumpelstiltskin*. (Dutton, 1986)

Zemach, Harve. *Duffy and the Devil*. Illustrated by Margot Zemach. (Farrar, Straus & Giroux, 1973)

Marianne J. Dyson—Saffron Chicken

At my grocery store, I picked up a flier about the Children's Institute of Literature's correspondence course on writing for children. I decided to give it a try.... My instructor encouraged me to use my science background to write nonfiction.

—Marianne J. Dyson

Marianne J. Dyson

Birthday: December 24

Favorite place: On the sofa beside my husband and cat; and the moon (There's a "Dyson crater on the far side!), on Earth (somewhere where I haven't been before).

Favorite foods: potato chips, Almond Joy, A&W Cream Soda, avocados, dates, yams, oranges

Family:

    Spouse—Thor

    Sons—Thomas and Scott

Home:

    Childhood—Canton, Ohio

    Now—Houston, Texas

Many of Marianne Dyson's growing up days were spent in Canton, Ohio, where she was born but her parents divorced when she was eleven so as a teenager she spent summers with her mother in various towns in Ohio, Pennsylvania, and North Carolina. She always had an interest in science, and after her undergraduate college work she accepted a fellowship in space physics and astronomy at Rice University and moved to Houston, Texas. Eventually she went to work for NASA, becoming one of the first ten women to work in Mission Control. She no longer works in the space industry but spends her time helping readers learn more about science through her writing. She and her husband own a small plane and have flown all over the United States together. She says, "Someday we hope to get our own spaceship and fly to the moon!"

Pineapple Sweet Yams

Preheat oven to 400° F. Place approximately 3 pounds of small unpeeled sweet potatoes (yams) on a baking sheet and bake for 1 hour or until tender. Cool for 15 minutes. Slice off an oval "lid" from each potato and carefully scoop pulp into a bowl (leave potato shell intact).

Mash the pulp and then stir in:

- 1/2 cup golden raisins
- 1 tablespoon light brown sugar
- 1/4 teaspoon ground cinnamon
- 1 8-ounce can crushed pineapple in own juice, drained
- 1 teaspoon vanilla extract

Spoon mixture back into the shells. Sprinkle with:

- 2 tablespoons chopped pecans
- 1 cup miniature marshmallows

Bake at 350° F for 15 minutes or until thoroughly heated.

NASA

Congress and President Dwight Eisenhower of the United States created the National Aeronautics and Space Administration (NASA) on October 1, 1958. NASA has provided research for flight within and outside the Earth's atmosphere since that time. The research benefited the space travel effort, but common citizens have also benefited from that research. Products and innovations include the following:

- Baby formula additive (Formulaid)—increases mental and visual development
- Ski boots with warmers built in—used heating element circuitry developed to keep astronauts warm or cool in extremes of the Moon
- Impedance cardiography—a technique to monitor heart function electronically
- Scratch-resistant lenses
- Water purification system using iodine
- Ribbed fabric used to reduce friction and aerodynamic drag, now used for competition swimsuits.
- Golf Ball Aerodynamics
- Athletic shoes with shock absorption.
- Forest management—a scanning system to detect radiation reflected and emitted from trees.

- Voice-controlled wheelchair
- Storm-warning services (Doppler radar)
- Lead poison detection
- Corrosion protection coating
- Robotic hands

   "Space is my passion and what I write about most. Each of my books have contained recipes related to space. But I don't live on the space frontier, not yet anyway, so what connection is there between my writing about space and my dinners here on Earth? Time and ingredients! People on the space frontier will not be able to grow a large variety of foods, and items imported from Earth will be expensive. They will have to cook from scratch and find creative ways to vary their menus. Time and power will always be in short supply, so cooking needs to be simple and fast. With food allergies and frequent deadlines, I face the same constraints. So what does a space writer or pioneer do when they look up from their latest project and discover it is past dinnertime and the children are starving? Pizza and fast food are not options."

—Marianne J. Dyson

So what does she do? She makes one of her "deadline dinners" that take 20 minutes from start to serving and contains no milk or eggs. One of her "deadline dinners" is Saffron Chicken.

Saffron Chicken

- 1 five-ounce bag of Mahatma Yellow Saffron Rice
- 3 boneless chicken thighs
- 1 small can mushrooms (or fresh if available)
- 1/4 cup onion, chopped
- 1/4 cup raisins
- 1–2 teaspoons salt
- 2 tablespoons oil
- 1 2/3 cups hot tap water

Crocus Sativus

Put rice pot and frying pan on the stove and pour 1 tablespoon of oil in each. Heat to medium high. Add the hot tap water, rice, and raisins to the pot. Bring to a boil and then reduce to simmer and cook for 20 minutes with the lid on. Cut chicken into cubes and place in frying pan. Sprinkle with salt. Add onions and mushrooms. Stir frequently until chicken is white and onions clear. When the rice is done, add the chicken mixture to it and stir. (Serves 2–3; Recipe can be doubled to serve a family of 4 or 5.)

Selected Books Written by Marianne J. Dyson

Home on the Moon: Living on a Space Frontier. (National Geographic, 2003)

Space Station Science: Life in Free Fall. (Scholastic, 1999)

Learning More about Space

In addition to reading the space books by Marianne Dyson you might want to read these books.

Aldrin, Buzz. *Reaching for the Moon.* Illustrated by Wendell Minor. (HarperCollins, 2005)

Brain, Marshall. *What If? How Stuff Works.* (Wiley, 2003)

Carlisle, Rodney P. *Exploring Space.* (Facts on File, 2004)

Stone, Tanya Lee. *Ilan Ramon, Israel's First Astronaut.* Millbrook Press, 2003.

Kathy Feeney—Marco Polo Bars

He tasted a nut "the size of a man's head and as white as milk." It was called a coconut. Marco ate a fruit called a date that grew on a palm tree. He tasted spices like nutmeg and ginger that were used to flavor food.

—from *Marco Polo: Explorer of China* **by Kathy Feeney**

Kathleen Frances Feeney

Birthday: July 3

Favorite place: The Library

Favorite foods: Lobster and Italian food

Family:

Spouse—R.J. Kwap

Pets—Dogs, Maxwell Smart and Miss Muggle

Home:

Childhood—Born in Providence, Rhode Island, but spent childhood in many places as father was in the army.

Now—Tampa, Florida

Books provided a refuge as Kathy Feeney moved to many places during her childhood. Her father was a member of the military and her childhood "was not perfect." But her love of writing developed and after graduating from high school, she entered the University of South Florida in Tampa where she earned a degree in journalism. For twenty years she was a newspaper reporter and staff writer for the *Stamford* (Connecticut) *Advocate* and later for the *Tampa Tribune*. As a travel writer she has traveled all over the world, including such locales as Australia, China, Iceland, Israel, France, Germany, Jamaica, Norway, and South Africa. Today she is a freelance travel writer and frequently travels on location for major publications. She also uses her research skills and her love of information to create children's information books. Since 1996, twenty-five of her books have been published. Today she writes and works from her Tampa, Florida, home that she shares with her husband R.J. and their two cats.

Marco Polo is said to have introduced pasta to Italy and thus sparked the firm bond between Italian cooking and pasta of all sorts. However, there's evidence suggesting the Etruscans made pasta as early as 400 B.C. Marco Polo wrote of eating Chinese pasta in his book about his travels but probably was not the first; a Genoan soldier listed *bariscella peina de macarone,* a small basket of macaroni, among his inventoried goods. The soldier's will (and inventory) is dated 1279, sixteen years before Marco Polo returned from China.

MarcoRoni

This recipe combines the pasta associated with Italian cooking and the garlic and onion utilized in early Chinese dishes.

Mix together and set aside:

- 1 cup chopped pine nuts
- 1/4 cup chopped black olives
- 1/4 cup chopped roasted red peppers
- 1/4 cup chopped fresh basil leaves
- 1/4 cup chopped red onion
- 1/4 cup diced plum tomatoes
- 1 clove minced garlic, sautéed until caramelized

You will also need:

- 8 ounces uncooked macaroni
- 1/4 cup olive oil
- 2 tablespoons balsamic vinegar
- salt and pepper
- parmesan or asiago cheese, grated

Cook 8 ounces macaroni according to package directions (al dente) and drain well. Toss the pasta with olive oil and vinegar, and season with salt and pepper. Spoon pine-nut mixture over macaroni and toss lightly at the table. Top each serving with grated parmesan or asiago cheese. (Serves 4)

Pasta * Pasta * Pasta

dePaola, Tomie. *Strega Nona*. (Simon & Schuster, 1975)

Gelman, Rita Golden. *More Spaghetti, I Say!* (Hello Reader, Level 2). Illustrated by Mort Gerberg. (Scholastic, 1993, reissue)

Sayre, April Pulley. *Noodle Man: The Pasta Superhero*. Illustrated by Stephen Costanza. (Orchard Books, 2002)

Wright, Alexandra. *Alice in Pastaland: A Math Adventure*. (Charlesbridge, 1997)

Although a few people traveled to unknown places, most people in Europe during the Middle Ages, spent their entire lives in the village where they were born. But in the thirteenth century, a seventeen-year-old Italian named Marco Polo traveled all the way to China! He spent seventeen years as a member of the court of Mongol emperor Kublai Khan. After he returned to Italy, he recorded his experiences in a book, sparking a surge in interest in the Far East among Europeans that led to a great age of exploration. Explorers brought back spices (nutmeg, cinnamon, ginger) and fruits, silk, and other goods unknown to the Europeans. Marco Polo died in 1324.

Marco Polo Bars

Marco Polo is said to have brought back coconuts and spices such as nutmeg and cloves. This recipe includes each of those—for a deliciously interesting taste.

- 1/2 cup butter
- 2 1/4 cups graham cracker crumbs
- 3 tablespoons sugar
- 21 ounces sweetened condensed milk
- 12 ounces semisweet chocolate chips
- 2 cups sweetened coconut, toasted

1 cup chopped dried fruit (apricots and cherries work well, chop with a food processor), tossed in ground cinnamon and ground nutmeg to taste.

Preheat oven to 350° F. (If using a glass pan, lower temperature to 325° F). Melt butter directly in a 13 x 9 inch pan. Sprinkle graham cracker crumbs and sugar over butter, mix, and press into pan (making a graham cracker crust). Spread toasted coconut on the crust. Pour sweetened condensed milk evenly over the coconut and crust. Top with chips and dried fruit. Press down firmly. Bake for 20 to 25 minutes until dry at the edges. Watch carefully so that edges do not get brown.

Selected Books Written by Kathy Feeney

Alabama. (Children's Press, 2002)

Black Bears (Our Wild World Series). Illustrated by John F. McGee. (Northword, 2000)

Davy Crockett: A Photo-Illustrated Biography. (Bridgestone, 2002)

Get Moving: Tips on Exercise. (Bridgestone, 2002)

Koalas for Kids (Wildlife for Kids Series). Illustrated by John F. McGee. (Northword, 2000)

Leopards (Our Wild World Series). Illustrated by John F. McGee. (Northword, 2002)

Manatees. Illustrations by John F. McGee. (Northword Press, 2001)

Marco Polo: Explorer of China (Enslow, 2004)

Martin Luther King, Jr.: A Photo-Illustrated Biography. (Bridgestone, 2002)

Rhode Island Facts and Symbols (Capstone Press, 2003). See also her other books in the series focusing on Tennessee, Puerto Rico, Utah, Vermont, Washington, D.C., South Dakota, West Virginia.

Sharp Shooters: 12 of Nature's Most Amazing. (Northword Press, 2001)

More Information about Marco Polo

Brandon, Alex. *The Travels of Marco Polo.* (Raintree/Steck-Vaughn, 2000)

Burgan, Michael. *Marco Polo and the Silk Road to China.* (Compass Point Books, 2002)

Herbert, Janis. *Marco Polo for Kids: His Marvelous Journey to China.* (Chicago Review Press, 2001)

MacDonald, Fiona. *The World in the Time of Marco Polo.* (Chelsea House, 2000)

Major, John S. *The Silk Route.* (HarperTrophy, 1996)

Strathloch, Robert. *Marco Polo.* (Heinemann, 2002)

Debra Frasier—Orange Ambrosia

Photo: Sharron L. McElmeel

On the day you were born / a forest of tall trees / collected the Sun's light / in their leaves, / where, in silent mystery, / they made oxygen / for you to breathe....

—from *On the Day You Were Born* by Debra Frasier

Debra Frasier

Birthday: April 3

Favorite place: Paddling on any river, rain or shine!

Favorite foods: Fresh cut navel orange

Family:

  Spouse—James Henkel, photographer and associate professor, University of Minnesota

  Daughter—Calla Henkel, a paper collage and fabric artist

Home:

  Childhood—Vero Beach, Florida

  Now—Minneapolis, Minnesota (considers Florida her "home state" though she has lived in Minnesota for twenty-one

---

While photographing *Out of the Ocean,* Debra Frasier lost two cameras. *Out of the Ocean* became an ocean journal documenting items found on the beach. Frasier had grown up on oceanfront property that her parents purchased in 1958, just north of Vero Beach, Florida. As an adult she returned often. She worked on the journal for five years—the day she finished the last entry for the book—April 25, 1995—Frasier's mother called to tell her that they had found a buyer for the family beach homestead. Ideas for each of her books come from within her own experiences. The birth of her daughter, Calla, inspired *On the Day You Were Born.* It was Calla, who at age nine, declared that she had figured out that Miss Alaineus was not a person.

Frasier says, "Vero Beach is at the heart of the Indian River Fruit grove country. My grandparents had a very small grove on the western edge of town, and when Thanksgiving and Christmas arrived, all of us piled into a big red station wagon loaded with empty boxes and headed to the grove. We bumped down dirt roads, turning between lines of trees heavy with giant navel oranges. The spider webs were *huge*, and we brought a broom to help fight our way through. We would make a long chain of people from a tree to an empty box on the tailgate of the car and throw an orange from the tree to the box, hand to hand. Ambrosia—the mix of cut navel oranges, pineapple, walnuts and coconut was my very, very favorite food. I learned to make ambrosia with the family recipe, and then learned that I liked just plain old oranges ... best of all."

Oranges in Books

 Debra Frasier's favorite food is "just a plain old orange." Enjoy one while sharing one of these books.

Ada, Alma Flor. *Three Golden Oranges*. (Atheneum, 1999; a classic Spanish folktale, retold)

Giganti, Paul. *Each Orange Had 8 Slices*. Illustrated by Donald Crews. (HarperTrophy, 1992)—mathematics

Lember, Barbara Hirsch. *A Book of Fruit*. (Ticknor & Fields, 1994; a book about growing fruit)

Partridge, Elizabeth. *Oranges on Golden Mountain*. Illustrated by Aki Sogabe. (Dutton, 2001; a story that tells of Chinese immigration, set in a California orange grove)

Polacco, Patricia. *An Orange for Frankie*. (Philomel, 2004; a Christmas tale)

Water * Water * Water

Debra Frasier's *The Incredible Water Show* examines the role of water in our life. These books examine water from other perspectives.

Base, Graeme. *The Waterhole*. (Putnam, 2004; a book focusing on the environment)

Branley, Franklyn M. *Down Comes the Rain* (Let's-Read-and-Find-Out Science, Stage 2). Illustrated by James Graham Hale. (HarperCollins, 1997; a book about the water cycle)

Kurtz, Jane. *River Friendly, River Wild*. Illustrated by Neil Brennan. (Simon & Schuster, 2000; tells of the negative effects of too much water)

Robinson, Tom. *The Everything Kids' Science Experiments Book: Boil Ice, Float Water, Measure Gravity—Challenge the World Around You!* (Everything Kids Series) (Adams Media, 2001; a collection of experiments)

Speed, Toby. *Water Voices*. Illustrated by Julie Downing. (Putnam, 1998; poems and riddles)

Yolen, Jane. *Water Music*. Illustrated by Jason Stemple. (Boyds Mills, 1995; a collection of poems)

Ambrosia

Ambrosia was known as the "food of the Gods," on Mount Olympus, and along with nectar was thought to be the food and drink of eternal life. Recipes for ambrosia began to appear in American cookbooks during the last quarter of the nineteenth century. A true ambrosia included dried coconut as an ingredient, a popular addition in the 1800s. Basically, the dessert is made from fruits, especially oranges, sugar, and grated coconut—most popular in the South. Sometimes bananas, cherries, and other fruits are included. Some cooks fold the fruit into whipped cream and add miniature marshmallows to make the salad a very sweet dessert dish.

Ambrosia Cake—Oranges and Coconut

In a large mixing bowl, combine the following ingredients: *Recipe*
- 1 tablespoon grated orange zest (grated rind of orange)
- 1/4 cup vegetable oil • 2 egg yolks • 6 tablespoons water
- 1/2 teaspoon vanilla extract • 1/2 cup flaked coconut

Add:
- 1 cup plus 2 tablespoons sifted cake flour
- 3/4 cup granulated sugar • 1 1/2 teaspoons baking powder

Set aside.

Beat until stiff peaks form:
- 4 egg whites • 1/2 teaspoon salt • 1/4 teaspoon cream of tartar

Fold the beaten egg whites into the first mixture. Mix gently but thoroughly. Pour batter into an ungreased square 8 x 8 x 2–inch baking pan or an 8-inch round cake pan. Bake at 350° F for about 30 minutes. Cool upside down for 1 hour. Loosen from pan and split horizontally into two layers. Between the layers, place a generous layer of whipped topping or sweetened whipped cream. Top the cake with another layer of whipped topping. Sprinkle with flaked coconut. Garnish with slices of orange.

Ambrosia

Combine:

- 1 cup orange juice
- 3 medium oranges, peeled and sectioned
- 1 can (8 ounces) pineapple chunks, undrained
- 1/2 cup seedless red grapes, halved

Stir gently to blend. Refrigerate until serving time. Just before serving, fold in:

- 1/2 cup shredded coconut
- 1/2 cup chopped walnuts

Serves 6.

Booklist

Selected Books Written by Debra Frasier

The Incredible Water Show. (Harcourt, 2004)

Miss Alaineus: A Vocabulary Disaster. (Harcourt, 2000)

On the Day You Were Born. (Harcourt, 1991)

Out of the Ocean. (Harcourt, 1998)

Susan Gaber—Cucumbers

Susan Gaber

Birthday: June 23

Favorite place: Home

Favorite foods: Fresh mozzarella and home baked baklava

Family:

Husband and son

Home:

Childhood—Brooklyn, New York

Now—New York

Ten little sheep/leap the cucumber vine./ Long grass bends./Spider mends./Sleep sheep.

—from *Ten Sleepy Sheep* by Phyllis Root

"My mom worked full time once my sister and I were in school. Dinners were simple and easy in order to cut down on shopping, preparation, and clean up. In reaction to frozen, boxed, and canned foods, at an appropriate life passage, I rebelled and became interested in baking things from scratch. I began baking bread when I was a teenager, later I was making my own tofu, and even later, I became interested in foods from other cultures and using food as a healing element to treat illnesses.

Shortly after meeting my husband, I abandoned an attempt I had made at vegetarianism. My husband had certain food sensitivities, and he didn't seem suited for the non-meat life-style. (In other words, he wasn't very enthusiastic when it came to vegetables.) I married him anyway because, among many other good qualities, he loved animals as much as I did.

A few years ago I decided it was important for me to give up eating meat again. Happily, it has been an easy transition. We all eat the same vegetables and carbohydrates, but I will prepare a meat entrée for my family and a vegetarian one for myself.

My husband and I enjoy gardening and every summer we grow our own vegetables. We enjoy having a few varieties of tomatoes, eggplants, peppers, zucchini, radishes, beans, lettuce, herbs, winter squash, turnips, cabbage, and broccoli. In 2004, for the first time, I grew pickling cucumbers. I think I might have been inspired after illustrating Phyllis Root's verse from *Ten Sleepy Sheep.*

—Susan Gaber

93

Baklava

This favorite food of Susan Gaber takes several steps to complete, but it is easy enough to make for a cultural-awareness event (Baklava is Greek and Middle Eastern in origin), a fundraiser, or any special event.

Purchase 1 package of frozen phyllo dough (16 ounces) thawed (overnight in the refrigerator or minimum of 6 hours). Do not thaw at room temperature as the dough will stick together.

Melt 1 1/2 cups (3 sticks) of butter.

Combine and set aside:

- 1 pound walnuts, finely chopped
- 1/2 cup sugar
- 2 teaspoons cinnamon

Lightly butter the bottom and sides of a jelly roll pan (approx. 15 x 10 x 1 inch)

Open the phyllo dough and layer 6 whole leafs in the pan (may overlap the pan).

Butter each layer as you put it down.

Spread 1 cup of the walnut mixture on top of the leaves.

Cut the remaining sheets in half and begin laying 8 half sheets, buttering between each sheet. The half sheets will not cover the pan completely, so stagger the placement of the sheets from corner to corner; to cover the entire pan overlapping where possible.

Spread another 1 cup of the walnut mixture.

Repeat 8 sheets and walnut mixture twice. You will end up with 4 layers of nuts.

Layer the remaining half sheets on top; butter each layer.

Brush the top with the remaining butter.

Trim off the edges.

Before baking, cut halfway through the layers making diamond-shaped pieces.

Bake 1 hour or until golden brown.

While the baklava is baking, combine in a saucepan:

- 1 cup sugar
- 1 cup water
- 1 tablespoon lemon juice

Begin to cook the sauce 15 minutes before the baking is scheduled to be completed. Cook sauce over a medium heat, stirring occasionally for 15 minutes.

Remove the sauce from the heat and add:

- 1 cup honey (net weight 12 ounces)
- 1/2 teaspoon vanilla

Remove the baklava from the oven and finish cutting through the layers. Pour the sauce over the hot baklava. Cool. Let it sit for at least 24 hours (lightly covered unrefrigerated).

Susan Gaber

Susan Gaber was born in Brooklyn, New York, in the mid-1950s and after earning an undergraduate degree, in 1978, from Long Island College she began her career as a freelance illustrator. Her attention turned to children's books in the 1980s. After her marriage in 1988, she continued her illustrative career as she raised her son. Susan Gaber uses watercolors and acrylics most often to create her illustrations. Using a folk style, her illustrations are often rendered in a jewel-tone palette. Gaber's interests outside of books and reading include gardening and the therapeutic use of herbs in treatments and diet (herbology).

Vinegar Cucumbers and Onions

Peel and slice 2 or 3 large cucumbers.

Soak cucumbers in salt water for 2 or 3 hours (refrigerated).

Peel and slice 1 large onion (more if you really like onions).

Rinse cucumbers thoroughly.

Put cucumbers and onion slices into a glass bowl (with cover) and cover with vinegar (add pepper to taste). Chill for 2 to 3 hours. Serve cold.

Yogurt and Mustard Seed Cucumbers

Whisk 2 cups plain nonfat yogurt until creamy. Then add:

- 1 teaspoon salt
- 1/8 teaspoon fresh ground black pepper
- 1/4 teaspoon crushed red pepper
- 4 tablespoons finely minced fresh cilantro
- 2 teaspoons whole black mustard seed, lightly ground
- 2 large cucumbers, peeled, chop in small pieces or grate coarsely.

Mix well and chill. Serve cold.

Selected Books Illustrated by Susan Gaber

The Finest Horse in Town. Text by Jacqueline Briggs Martin. (HarperCollins, 1992; Purple House Press, 2003)

Good Times on Grandfather Mountain. Text by Jacqueline Briggs Martin. (Orchard Books, 1992)

The Language of Birds. Text by Rafe Martin. (Putnam, 2000)

Small Talk. Text by Lee Bennett Hopkins. (Harcourt, 1995)

Stone Soup. Text by Heather Forest. (August House, 1998)

Ten Sleepy Sheep. Text by Phyllis Root. (Candlewick, 2004)

When Winter Comes. Text by Nancy Van Laan. (Atheneum, 2000)

Cucumbers to Pickles

Barrett, Judi. *Pickles to Pittsburgh.* (Aladdin, 2000)

Bradfield, Jolly Roger. *Pickle-Chiffon Pie.* (Purple House Press, 2004)

Kennedy, Frances. *The Pickle Patch Bathtub.* Illustrations by Sheila Aldridge. (Tricycle Press, 2004)

Terban, Marvin. *In a Pickle and Other Funny Idioms.* (Clarion, 1983)

Gail Gibbons—Apple Pie

Photo: Kent Antcliffe

Arnold and his family make apple pies with apples from Arnold's apple tree.

—from *The Seasons of Arnold's Apple Tree* by Gail Gibbons

Gail Gibbons

Birthday: August 1

Favorite place: Our pond on our property in Vermont.

Favorite foods: Salads, fruit, popcorn, pies, and cakes

Family:

   Spouse—Kent Ancliffe

   Son—Eric Ancliffe

   Daughter—Rebecca Buttignol (married to Roger; mother of Gail's first grandchild, Greta)

Home:

   Childhood—Oak Park, Illinois

   Now—Corinth, Vermont

Gail Gibbons's career in children's books began in the mid-1970s, and she evolved as the foremost author of informational picture books. She has written more than 120 books for young readers and has written titles on everything from honeybees to quilting. Gibbons grew up in Illinois, and after working for a time in Chicago she moved to Manhattan and later to a three-hundred-acre farm in Vermont. There she and her husband raised Rebecca and Eric. It was Eric and his special relationship with an old apple tree that sat on a hilltop near their home in Corinth that inspired *The Seasons of Arnold's Apple Tree*. The tree is Arnold's (Eric's) special place and readers view the tree through all four seasons—from bare branches, blossoms, and ripened fruit.

"Quite a while ago I had a book come out called *The Seasons of Arnold's Apple Tree*. It's really a true story of what my son did with an apple tree on a hill where I live in Vermont. The book has a page that has an apple pie recipe. This book has been in print for a long time. We planted a beautiful apple orchard next to our pond in Vermont about three years ago. The apple tree in my book was a very old apple tree."

—**Gail Gibbons**

In *Marge's Diner* Marge serves up great food and a homey environment. In her books, Gail Gibbons serves up some great food ideas too. Besides the apple pie recipe, Gibbons included instructions for growing strawberries and recipes for blueberry pie, blackberry jam, and raspberry ice cream in *The Berry Book*. Readers will find many other connections to make: wonderful recipes with honey (*The Honey Makers)* and delicious egg dishes (*Chicks and Chickens)*, and just think of the wonderful potluck dishes one could bring to a quilting bee (*Quilting Bee)*.

Bumbleberry Pie

Based on Gail Gibbon's *The Berry Book.*

Prepare two recipes of the pie pastry; and line two, 9-inch pie pans with pastry.

To make filling, combine:

- 2 cups sugar
- 2/3 cup flour
- 2 tablespoons lemon juice
- 2 cups fresh or frozen blueberries
- 2 cups fresh or frozen raspberries
- 2 cups fresh or frozen strawberries
- 2 cups fresh or frozen blackberries

Split filling between the 2 pie shells and top with second crust and cut vents. Mix 1 egg yolk with a little water and brush on crusts. Sprinkle top with a sprinkling of white sugar. Or if you prefer not to use a top crust, bake without and then garnish before serving with a dollop of whipped topping and a single berry in the middle. Bake at 350° F for 50 to 60 minutes.

Pie Pastry

Make pie crust dough:

Mix 1 3/4 cups of all-purpose flour and 1 teaspoon salt into a mixing bowl.

Cut in 1/3 cup of cold, solid butter.

Mix with a fork until each piece of the butter is smaller than a kernel of corn.

Add 1/3 cup of ice cold water, a tablespoon at a time.

Mix until you can make a ball of dough. Divide in half. Roll one portion of the ball into a circle 1/8 inch thick. Smooth it into a 9-inch pie pan. Make sure the edges of the dough stick above the edge of the pie pan.

Filling: Make filling according to directions for your selected pie.

Top pie layer: Roll the second crust out in the same manner as above and prepare to use it as the top crust for your pie.

Arnold's Apple Pie

(Adapted)

Make one recipe of pie pastry dough. Line one 9-inch pie pan with pie pastry.

Prepare apple filling:

Core and slice 6 to 8 apples.

Put the slices into the pastry lined pie pan.

Mix:

- 1/2 cup brown sugar
- 1/4 teaspoon salt
- 1/2 teaspoon cinnamon
- 1/4 teaspoon nutmeg

Sprinkle the mixture over the apples.

Apples should form a mound in the center of the pan, rising 1–2 inches above the top of the pan. Lay the top crust over the apples, and smooth it down. Crimp the edges of the top crust to the edge of the bottom crust, and trim any excess dough from the crimped edge. Use a sharp knife to cut six 1-inch slits on the top crust. Mix 1 egg yolk with a little water and brush on crusts. Sprinkle top with a sprinkling of white sugar. Bake in a preheated oven for 50 minutes at 425°.

Signature Recipe—Gail Gibbons

Selected Books Written/Illustrated by Gail Gibbons

The Berry Book. (Holiday House, 2002)

Chicks and Chickens. (Holiday House, 2003)

Giant Pandas. (Holiday House, 2002)

Grizzly Bear. (Holiday House, 2003)

The Honey Makers. (HarperCollins, 1997)

Horses. (Holiday House, 2003)

Marge's Diner. (Crowell, 1989)

Mummies, Pyramids, and Pharaohs. (Little, Brown, 2004)

Quilting Bee. (HarperCollins, 2004)

Tell Me, Tree. (Little Brown, 2002)

Thanksgiving Is ... (Holiday House, 2004)

The Seasons of Arnold's Apple Tree. (Harcourt, 1984)

Apple Books

Arnold, Katya. *That Apple Is Mine!* Illustrated by V. Suteev. (Holiday House, 2000)

Brunelle, Lynn. *Bite into an Apple.* Illustrated by Jacqueline A. Ball. (Blackbirch Press, 2003)

Bryant, Megan E. *A Is for Apple: And All Things That Grow!* (Grosset & Dunlap, 2002)

Cheripko, Jan. *Brother Bartholomew and the Apple Grove.* Illustrated by Kestutis Kasparavicius. (Boyds Mills, 2004)

Gibbons, Gail. *Apples.* (Holiday House, 2000)

Hubbell, Will. *Apples Here*! (Whitman, 2002)

Purmell, Ann. *Apple Cider Making Days.* (Millbrook Press, 2002)

Robbins, Ken. *Apples.* (Atheneum, 2002)

Wellington, Monica. *Apple Farmer Annie.* (Dutton, 2001)

Paul Goble—Buffalo Berry Preserves

What are Buffalo Berries? An ornamental plant (Shepherdia argentea)—a very thorny and hardy, large shrub or small tree. Foliage is silvery and ornamental. The scarlet fruits have silver scales on them and are used in jellies, jams, dried or eaten raw.

"Buffalo Berries, which grow in some places on the Great Plains are really only sweet enough when picked in the Fall after the first few frosts. People do not know this, and hardly bother with them, and also because the bushes guard their fruit with terrible sharp thorns, making it nigh impossible to pick them.

"Each year my mother- and father-in-law would nevertheless painfully pick a precious few berries and make them into the most delicious jelly. From my research I knew how Native Americans picked Buffalo Berries. I had written and illustrated the story of Iktomi and the Berries. Iktomi, the rascally trickster, had been drinking at a stream one hot day when he saw berries in the water. Not being a very bright person, he never realized that he was seeing a reflection of the bushes above his head. He dived in and nearly drowned in his search for the reflected fruit. Finally lying exhausted on the bank, he saw the fruit above his head. He was so angry that he beat the bushes with a stick to punish them:

Iktomi beating the Buffalo Berries from the bushes with a stick from *Iktomi and the Buffalo Berries* by Paul Goble (Orchard, 1989). Used with permission.

" 'Take that!—and that—and THAT! You brainless berry bushes. Don't you ever dare to try and trick me like that again! DO YOU HEAR ME? From now on everyone will beat you when they pick your berries.'

"My wife, Janet, and our son, Robert, took sheets and spread them under the Buffalo Berry bushes close to Slim Buttes in South Dakota, and gently beat the branches. Within half an hour we had more fruit in a box (together with the most beautiful green spiders) than my dear mother-in-law had seen in her entire fruit-picking life!

"Buffalo Berries make the most beautiful colored, and flavored jelly, with a faint tartness. Two pints of fruit to one of sugar are, I think, the usual amounts for jelly making."

—**Paul Goble**

Photo: Janet Goble

Paul Goble

Birthday: September 27

Favorite foods: Indian foods

Family:

    Spouse—Janet

    Sons—Richard, Robert

    Daughter—Julia

Home:

    Childhood—Surrey, England

    Now—South Dakota

Paul Goble

From the time he was young in England, Paul Goble has been fascinated by Native American culture. The interest persisted through his college years—where he studied to be an industrial engineer—and through his military service. His love of Native American culture was an avocation and eventually, through his art and writing, the Native American culture became entwined with his vocation. After searching for Native American books for his two oldest children, Richard and Julia, he decided that someone needed to write accurate accounts of historical events from the Native American perspective. Goble spent many summers on reservations in South Dakota and Montana. He and his first wife, Dorothy Goble, coauthored several books about Native Americans before Goble moved to the United States in 1977.

In 1978, Goble married Janet Tiller and settled in the Black Hills of South Dakota. He continued to study Native American culture, meeting with people on the reservations, attending ceremonies, and visiting historical museums to study paintings and beadwork. For a few years in the early 1990s, the Gobles moved to New York to be near their son, Robert, while he attended boarding school. They eventually moved back to the Plains—first to Montana and Nebraska, and then back home in the Black Hills.

In addition to his historical books, his most popular titles include those about the Plains Indian trickster, Iktomi (eek-TOE-me). He is mischievous and has magical powers, but he is also not too smart and is untruthful. Iktomi often attempts to outsmart others but more often ends up being outsmarted himself. Goble strives to instill a sense of pride in Native American children regarding their culture. In the Iktomi tales, he also attempts to bring the trickster from the past to the present by featuring Iktomi in jogging clothes or as he did in one scene, by featuring him in a T-shirt that declared, "I'm Sioux and Proud of It."

Buffalo Berry Sweet and Sour Sauce

Combine the following ingredients in a saucepan and heat for 10 minutes:

- Grated rind of 1 orange   • 2 cups water   • 2 cups sugar

Add:

- 4 cups buffalo berries

Cook until berries pop.

Add and cook for an additional 5 minutes:

- 1/4 teaspoon ground cinnamon   • Pinch of ground cloves

Put mixture in a bowl and chill. Serve this red, spicy sauce cold on warm ham or grilled chicken breasts or turkey.

Buffalo Berry Preserves

Wash and stem:

- 1 quart ripe buffalo berries

Place in a large saucepan and bring to boil with:

- 1/2 cup cold water

Once the berries are thoroughly warmed, crush with a masher and bring to a boil.

Use a colander with its wooden pestle to press out the juice and pulp from the berries. Discard the pits and skins from the colander.

Measure the amount of berry and juice mixture you have. Then put the mixture back into the pan and add:

- 1 1/2 cups of sugar per cup of berry and juice mixture.

Mix well and bring to a boil.

Buffalo berries contain natural pectin, so they should gel naturally. Bring to a boil for 4 full minutes while stirring constantly. Skim off foam and pour into hot, sterile glass jars and seal.

Buffalo Berry Syrup: If you wish to have pancake and waffle syrup, cut the boiling to 1 minute and pour into containers before jelling takes place.

Selected Books Written/Illustrated by Paul Goble

The Girl Who Loved Wild Horses. (Bradbury, 1978: Atheneum/Richard Jackson Books, 2001; revised edition)

Iktomi and the Berries: A Plains Indian Story. (Orchard Books, 1989)

Iktomi and the Boulder: A Plains Indian Story. (Orchard Books, 1988)

Iktomi and the Buffalo Skull: A Plains Indian Story. (Orchard Books, 1991)

Iktomi and the Buzzard: A Plains Indian Story. (Orchard Books, 1994)

Iktomi and the Coyote: A Plains Indian Story. (Orchard Books, 1998)

Iktomi and the Ducks: A Plains Indian Story. (Orchard Books, 1990)

Iktomi Loses His Eyes: A Plains Indian Story. (Orchard, 1999)

The Legend of the White Buffalo Woman. (National Geographic Society, 1998)

Mystic Horse. (HarperCollins, 2003)

Paul Goble Gallery: Three Native American Stories. (Simon & Schuster, 1999; Includes: *Her Seven Brothers, The Gift of the Sacred Dog,* and *The Girl Who Loved Wild Horses*)

Snow Maker's Tipi. (Atheneum, 2001)

Song of Creation. (Eerdmans, 2004)

Carol Gorman—Spaghetti

My stomach growled, and I remembered I was so nervous about the tryouts, I hadn't eaten since breakfast. "What's for supper?"
"Spaghetti," Mom said.
"Good, Mom makes great spaghetti," I told Luther. I turned back to Mom. "Maybe can Luther stay for supper?"

—from *Stumptown Kid* by Carol Gorman and Ron Findley

Carol Gorman

Birthday: February 16

Favorite place: Favorite peaceful place—my backyard; favorite exciting place—Manhattan

Favorite foods: favorite guilty pleasure—chocolate mousse; favorite healthy food—tomato and basil sandwich

Family:

Spouse—Ed Gorman

Son—Ben Johnson

Home:

Childhood—Iowa City, Iowa

Now—Cedar Rapids, Iowa

Carol Gorman says that her main characters often "have a lot of me in them." When she speaks to young readers about Jerry Flack, the main character in her award-winning Dork books, she acknowledges that she was a dork during her growing up years. Some of her characters, such as Chelsey and Jack in *Chelsey and the Green-Haired Kid* have more nerve than she does. Most likely Carol would not have gone careening down Suicide Hill hanging onto a wheelchair as Jack does in that book. *Stumptown Kid*, while officially taking place in Holden, Iowa, has many locations that will be recognized by those familiar with the Midwestern town where she lives today.

Carol began her writing career while she was teaching language arts to middle school students. She married a fellow writer, Ed Gorman, who encouraged her to use her writing talents to write down her stories for publication. She did and one of her first articles, a story based on the parenting skills exhibited on the *Andy Griffith Show,* was published. Encouraged, she turned to writing books. Her first two books were nonfiction; and then she turned to mystery and suspense tales. She wrote two novels that did not sell, but her third was a success. *Chelsey and the Green-Haired Kid* became her first published mystery novel. Her insights into the life of a middle school learner brought her to write about Jerry Flack—a "dork" who wants to change his image at his new school. *Dork in Disguise* garnered five state awards, several more nominations, and spawned two sequels: *Dork on the Run* and *A Midsummer Night's Dork.* *Stumptown Kid* takes Gorman back to the mystery and suspense genre. Why did Luther, an African American, end up in Holden? What was his story? And what was his motivation for helping Charlie with his baseball skills?

Chocolate Mousse

Whip 2 pints of whipping cream and set aside in cool place. Beat 6 egg whites until they are stiff and set aside in cool place. Melt 8 ounces semisweet chocolate in the top of a double boiler. In another saucepan, combine:

- 2 cups lukewarm water
- 2 cups of sugar

Cook over low heat until sugar liquefies and is integrated into the water. Add the sugar syrup to the chocolate and beat. Gently fold the whipped cream into the egg whites. Beat chocolate again. If chocolate has thickened, add 1 more tablespoon water. Fold chocolate into cream and egg mixture, and spoon into individual glasses or cups. Chill. Makes 8 generous servings.

Spaghetti on a Shoestring

Prepare two cups of bread crumbs and set aside. Chop two large onions and two tomatoes. Begin cooking 1 package (500 grams) spaghetti according to the package directions. While spaghetti is cooking, heat one tablespoon oil in a saucepan. Add the chopped onions and braise over a low heat. Then add the tomatoes, cover, and let the mixture simmer until tomatoes are cooked. Salt and pepper to taste.

Grease an oven-proof dish and layer the bottom with 2/3 cup of bread crumbs.

Drain spaghetti.

Layer baking dish, on top of bread crumbs with tomato and onion mixture, then with spaghetti. Layer the bread crumbs, tomato and onion, and spaghetti again. The last layer will be just the bread crumbs. Dot with a bit of butter or margarine. Bake in the oven for approximately 15 minutes in a moderate oven.

(Optional: If you wish to add meat to the tomato and onion mixture, you may brown hamburger or ground turkey and add it to the simmering tomato and onions.)

Negro Baseball League

In Gorman's *Stumptown Kid*, one of the elements is the Negro Baseball League. Expand on the theme with one of these titles.

Golenbock, Peter. *Teammates.* (Gulliver, 1990)

McKissack, Pat, and Fredrick McKissack, Jr. *Black Diamond: The Story of the Negro Baseball Leagues.* (Polaris, 1998)

Ritter, Lawrence. *Leagues Apart: The Men and Times of the Negro Baseball Leagues.* Illustrated by Richard Merkin. (William Morrow, 1995)

Weatherford, Carole Boston. *A Negro League Scrapbook.* (Boyd Mills Press, 2005)

Selected Books Written/Illustrated by Carol Gorman

Chelsey and the Green-Haired Kid. (Houghton Mifflin, 1987; Perfection Learning, 2003)

Dork in Disguise. (HarperCollins, 1999)

Dork on the Run. (HarperCollins, 2002)

A Midsummer Night's Dork. (HarperCollins, 2004)

Stumptown Kid. (Peachtree, 2005)

Dan Gutman—Fruit

Drink lots of skim milk and fruit juice. That's it. Now get on with your life and concern yourself with problems that aren't so easy to solve.

—Dan Gutman

Dan Gutman

Birthday: October 19

Favorite place: New York City

Favorite foods: Chinese, roast chicken, and pizza

Family:

Spouse—Nina

Son—Sam

Daughter—Emma

Home:

Childhood—Newark, New Jersey

Now—Haddonfield, New Jersey

Dan Gutman never considered himself a good reader during his childhood, but he did enter Rutgers and earned a degree in psychology. Soon he determined that he was not really interested in working in that field—what he wanted to do was to be a writer. When he finally turned his writing efforts toward children's books, he wanted to be a different kind of writer—he wanted to appeal to the reluctant reader. His first effort was focused on adult audiences, but when his first child was born in 1990, he was exposed to children's books, and because his "writing for grown-ups was going nowhere, I decided to give children's books a try."

Dan's children's books have won several state awards and have hooked a variety of readers. He has become a prolific author—having published approximately four titles a year for young readers, many of them involving sports in some way. Gutman is able to attract the sports fan and entertain the reader with solid information about sports and a great deal of humor. He was able to parlay interest in baseball cards into a time-travel tale in which the holder of the card is transported back in time to a major incident in sports history. He has also written a mystery series, and books about the twelve-year-old who flew across the Atlantic Ocean, about iceskating, and about the Wright Brothers. When he is not traveling to schools to talk to and encourage readers, he writes every day and generally can write a book in two to four months. Readers are attracted to his books because they are filled with sports, mystery, weird school events, and a lot of humor.

BASEBALL FACTS—FACT OR FABLE?

Baseball was invented by Alexander Cartwright (1845).

The Cincinnati Red Stockings became the first professional (paid) baseball team (1869).

National Association of Professional Base Ball Players became the first professional baseball league (1871).

The first major league, the National League, was formed (1876).

Frederick Winthrop Thayer received a patent for a baseball catcher's mask on February 12, 1878.

A combined cap and baseball mitt patent (#4,768,232) was granted on September 6, 1988.

Abner Doubleday—a Civil War hero—invented baseball (1839).

A Word or Two from Dan Gutman

"I don't really cook, and to be honest, food is not really an important part of my life. I have always been skinny, and don't really take great pleasure in food the way most other people do. To me, it's just fuel to keep the car running. I'm always amazed by all these fad diets that come and go. … Seems to me the way to stay healthy is simple: eat moderate amounts of fruit, vegetables, nuts, fiber, and protein. Stay away from fat, processed food, and junk food. Treat yourself to a sweet every so often, but not every day."

—Dan Gutman

Dan Gutman says, "Drink lots of skim milk and fruit juice."

Orange Julius

- 1/2 cup orange juice
- 3/4 cup skim milk
- 1/2 teaspoon vanilla extract
- 1 packet artificial sweetener or 1 tablespoon sugar
- 4 ice cubes

Put all ingredients into blender and mix for a few minutes until ice cubes are crushed.

Fruit and Nut Salad

In a large bowl, combine the following and set aside:

- 1 large red apple, sliced thinly
- 1 large pear, sliced thinly
- 1 large orange, peeled and sliced

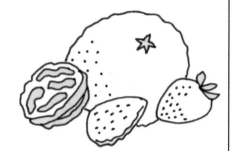

In a small bowl combine

- 1/3 cup vegetable oil
- 3 tablespoons white wine vinegar
- 1 tablespoon honey

Pour oil mixture over fruit, tossing to coat well.

Line six salad dishes with lettuce leaves.

Arrange fruit salad in each of the dishes.

Sprinkle each serving with a heaping teaspoon of chopped pecans or walnuts.

Baseball Cards–More Stories and Information

Erwin, Vicki Berger. *The Disappearing Card Trick.* (Elizabeth Bryan Mysteries, Book 1). (Concordia Press, 1996)

Preller, James, et al. *The Case of the Stolen Baseball Cards* (A Jigsaw Jones Mystery, Book 5). (Little Apple, 1999)

Preller, James. *The Major League Baseball Card Collector's Kit.* (Tangerine Press, 2003)

Skead, Robert. *Safe at Home: A Baseball Card Mystery.* (Cross Training, 1999)

Slote, Alfred. *The Trading Game.* (HarperCollins, 1992)

Selected Books Written by Dan Gutman

Babe Ruth and the Ice Cream Mess. Illustrated by Elaine Garvin. (Aladdin, 2004)

Baseball Card Adventures Series: *Honus & Me* (Avon, 1997); *Jackie & Me* (Avon, 1999); *Babe & Me* (HarperCollins, 2000); *Mickey & Me* (HarperCollins, 2003); *Abner & Me* (HarperCollins, 2005); *The Get Rich Quick Club.* (HarperCollins, 2004)

The Million Dollar Kick. (Hyperion, 2000)

The Million Dollar Shot. (Hyperion, 1997)

Qwerty Stevens, Stuck in time with Benjamin Franklin. (An Edison Mystery). (Simon & Schuster, 2002)

Shoeless Joe & Me. (HarperCollins, 2002)

Esther Hershenhorn—Chicken Soup

Photo: Kevin Hammett

With four books on the library shelves, I now know: cooking up a story is just like cooking chicken soup.

—Esther Hershenhorn

Esther Hershenhorn

Birthday: December 15

Favorite place: Wrigley Field and Lincoln Park Zoo

Favorite foods: mashed potatoes, stuffing, gravy, and roast turkey!

Family:

    Son—Jon

Home:

    Childhood—Philadelphia, Pennsylvania

    Now—Chicago, Illinois

"In the case of my picture book *Chicken Soup by Heart*, the first thing I simmered was a Chicago newspaper article titled 'The Great Chicken Soup Debate.' The author sought the ingredients for the World's Best Chicken Soup. Her Hungarian sister-in-law insisted on fresh tomatoes. Her friend from Minsk countered, 'Sweet peas! Add sweet peas!' A neighbor from Greece refuted, 'Lemons! You need lemons!' "

"So many cooks from so many places offered so many ingredients, the author's head spun.

"My head spun, too, once I began simmering that story idea. Month after month I savored bowls and pots of chicken soup while reading every chicken soup book ever written. I read recipes for clear broths, creamed soups, gumbos and tortilla soup, for Cock-a-leekie and mulligatawny. I read about roasters and broilers and the value of a capon. I studied medical reports likening chicken soup to penicillin.

"But the spinning was worth it. Before long, I'd cooked up a character, Rudie Dinkins, who shared his beloved babysitter Mrs. Gittel with eight little misters and misses in his Brooklyn apartment house. I'd cooked up a problem —Mrs. Gittel had the flu!—and eight loving chefs cooking Mrs. Gittel chicken soup. Of course, each chef cooked the chicken soup his or her family's way.

"In its final reduction, the story of friendship belonged to Rudie and Mrs. Gittel. Mrs. Gittel's chicken soup secret—she stirred in three very nice stories about her soon-to-be soup-eaters—proved good for the cook and good for the soup-eater."

—Esther Hershenhorn

Esther Hershenhorn

Esther Hershenhorn taught fifth-grade and gifted students in Chicago and its suburbs before turning her full attention to writing for young readers. Many of her books seem to take the reader on past the story and into a world that encourages more learning. For example, in *There Goes Lowell's Party!* the book integrates weather folklore into the story of a young boy who is anxiously waiting to see whether any of his relatives will make it to his party. Twenty-nine rain proverbs are added at the end of the book, beckoning curious readers to investigate the validity of each or to add more proverbs to the list.

> Throughout the illustrations for *There Goes Lowell's Party* Jacqueline Roger hid nineteen of the rain proverbs. Twins and triplets populate her illustrations along with surprised expressions, mustaches, and beards on the subjects of falling portraits.

In *The Confe$$ion$ and $ecret$ of Howard J. Fingerhut,* Hershenhorn was able to incorporate information about the critical elements for becoming a successful business person. She seems to always have an angle for more learning.

In *Chicken Soup by Heart,* Hershenhorn shares her recipe for chicken soup, but there are as many ways to make chicken soup as there are cooks. Here's a recipe for mulligatawny—an Indian dish that is the counterpart to chicken soup in that culture—a version of chicken soup that the author might have encountered in her quest for information relating to chicken soup. Some recipes use lamb instead of chicken and a variety of other vegetables. It is basically a stew.

Mulligatawny

Combine in a large soup pot:

- 6 cups chicken broth
- 1 (15.5 ounces) can chopped tomatoes
- 1 cup chopped celery
- 1 cup chopped tart apple
- 1/2 cup chopped carrots
- 2 tablespoons snipped parsley
- 3/4 cup chopped onions
- 2–3 teaspoons curry powder
- 1 1/2 teaspoons lemon juice
- 4 cups cooked, cubed chicken (precooked)
- 5 cups hot cooked rice

Slowly simmer all ingredients for an hour or two until all flavors are well blended. May be cooked in a slow cooker. Serve with fresh warm bread.

Homemade Chicken Soup

Coat the bottom of a large heavy-bottomed skillet with olive oil and sauté the breasts (from a whole chicken) in the pan until they are light brown. This will take about 5 minutes. After they are browned, remove and set aside.

Into the skillet add 1 onion, diced. Sauté until the onions are translucent (about 4–5 minutes). Remove the onions and set aside.

Cut the rest of the whole chicken into small pieces (use a meat cleaver or a sharp chef's knife.) Brown the pieces in the skillet and cook (on medium heat) until pieces are no longer pink.

Add the sautéed onions into the skillet and reduce heat to low, cover, and simmer until the chicken releases its juices, about 20 minutes.

In a large soup pot, heat 2–3 quarts of water to boiling, then add in:

- browned chicken breasts
- 2 teaspoons of salt
- 2 bay leaves

Cook for about 20 minutes and then remove whole chicken breasts from the pot and set aside.

Add in the rest of the chicken and onions and cook for 5 minutes. Remove pot from the stove and skim the fat from the broth.

Then add:

- 1 large carrot, peeled and sliced
- 1 celery stalk, sliced

When the chicken breasts are cool enough to handle, remove and discard the skin and bones. Shred the breast meat into bite sized pieces and add to the pot. Add 1/2 teaspoon dried thyme and simmer until the vegetables are tender.

Salt and pepper to taste. Garnish with 1/4 cup minced fresh parsley leaves.

Optional: Add in noodles (homemade or premade) or pasta shells and continue to cook until tender.

Selected Books Written by Esther Hershenhorn

There Goes Lowell's Party! Illustrated by Jacqueline Rogers. (Holiday House 1998)

Chicken Soup By Heart. Illustrated by Rosanne Litzinger. (Simon & Schuster 2002)

Fancy That. Illustrated by Megan Lloyd. (Holiday House 2003)

The Confe$$ion$ and $ecret$ of Howard J. Fingerhut. Illustrated by Ethan Long. (Holiday House, 2002)

Trina Schart Hyman and Katrin Tchana
—Sweet Rice Cakes

Photo: John Layton

Katrin Tchana (left) and
Trina Schart Hyman

Katrin Tchana

Birthday: May 2

Favorite place: the coast of Maine

Favorite foods: Asian food,
especially dumplings

Family:

　Mother—Trina Schart Hyman

　Sons—Michou (1989) and Xavier
　(1995)

Home

　Childhood—New Hampshire

　Now—West Fairlee, Vermont

The Serpent Slayer has several stories in which women use the power of well-prepared food to better their opponents and win the day. Throughout the ages preparing and serving food has been the special domain of women. A well-prepared meal is a powerful magic.

—Katrin Tchana

While Trina Schart Hyman was growing up, her mother made her a red satin cape and she spent an entire year wearing it. Her favorite story was "Little Red Riding Hood." Trina eventually grew up to become an acclaimed illustrator of children's books and created an illustrated version of that story. While working as an illustrator, she also raised her daughter Katrin who married a Cameroon prince and went off to live in Cameroon for several years. Now Katrin lives in Vermont with her two sons. So when Hyman wanted to represent a Vermont family, she used Katrin's two sons as models for the children that appear in *A Child's Calendar*—a book that earned Hyman a Caldecott Honor award. Katrin Tchana's and Trina Schart Hyman's first collaboration resulted in *The Serpent Slayer: and Other Stories of Strong Women*. Together they created two more titles before Hyman's death from cancer in November 2004.

Trina Schart Hyman (April 8, 1939–November 20, 2004)

Hyman's family included her life partner, Jean Aull; her daughter, Katrin Tchana; and two grandsons, Michou and Xavier. Hyman grew up in Wyncote, Pennsylvania, and lived in New England at the time of her death.

HONEY RICE CAKES TO DIE FOR!

Original drawing by Trina Schart Hyman.

About *The Serpent Slayer*

"My favorite food is Chinese food, and I've always wanted to visit China, mainly so I could eat Chinese food day and night. When I was working on *The Serpent Slayer* I lived in Burlington, Vermont, and my friend Xiu Ying, who is from China, used to come over a lot so that we could talk and her little daughter could play with my little son. While our kids were playing we would often make dumplings, which is a great way to pass time if you love to sit around and talk, which is my favorite activity next to eating. Xiu Ying gave me lots of advice on how to rewrite the title story in *The Serpent Slayer,* which is a folktale from China. I named the evil magician in that story after Xiu Ying's husband, Qi Fu. Xiu Ying's husband Qi Fu isn't really evil, he's a great guy, but Xiu Ying told me his name means "devious one," so I thought that was appropriate for the evil magician.

In the story of "The Serpent Slayer" the young girl Li Chi shows great courage and cleverness in battling the serpent which has eaten so many of her sisters. Li Chi tricks the terrible serpent, luring him out of his cave by cooking sweet rice cakes on a nearby rock. When the serpent lunges for the aromatic rice cakes, Li Chi seizes the moment and kills him with her sword. *The Serpent Slayer* has several stories in which women use the power of well-prepared food to better their opponents and win the day. Throughout the ages preparing and serving food has been the special domain of women. A well-prepared meal is a powerful magic."

—**Katrin Tchana**

PREPARING FOR THE FESTIVAL

The most significant holiday for ethnic Chinese is a fifteen-day festival that starts with the New Moon on the first day of the new year—during January and February. Families often gather together to prepare the New Year's cakes. Most Chinese cakes are steamed but these cakes are a baked, a Western version of the traditional cakes. These cakes can be made for any special occasion.

Chinese Rice Cakes

- 1 pound sweet rice flour
- 1 1/2 cups sugar
- 2 teaspoons baking powder
- 1 cup vegetable oil
- 4 medium eggs
- 1 can coconut milk or 1 1/2 c regular milk
- 1/8 cup chopped cilantro
- 1/4 cup minced onion, caramelized
- 1 can red bean paste
- 1 cup walnuts

Preheat oven to 350° F. Mix all ingredients together until smooth (except for bean paste and walnuts). Pour half of the mixture into a 9 x 11–inch pan and bake for 10 min. Then spread red bean paste into pan and cover with the rest of the mixture and walnuts. Return to oven for another 10–15 minutes. Cut into squares when cool. Excellent with stir-fried vegetables.

Selected Books Authored or Illustrated by Trina Schart Hyman or Katrin Tchana

Grimm Brothers. *Little Red Riding Hood*. Illustrated by Trina Schart Hyman. (Holiday House, 1983)

Hodges, Margaret. *Saint George and the Dragon*. Illustrated by Trina Schart Hyman. (Little, Brown, 1984)—Caldecott Award, 1985

Kimmel, Eric. *Hershel and the Hanukkah Goblins*. Illustrated by Trina Schart Hyman. (Holiday House, 1989)—Caldecott Honor, 1990.

Tchana, Katrin. *Goddesses Stories*. Illustrated by Trina Schart Hyman. (Scholastic, 2005)

Tchana, Katrin. *Sense Pass King: a Story from Cameroon*. Illustrated by Trina Schart Hyman. (Holiday House, 2002)

Tchana, Katrin. *The Serpent Slayer: and Other Stories of Strong Women*. Illustrated by Trina Schart Hyman. (Little, Brown, 2000)

Updike, John. *A Child's Calendar*. Illustrated by Trina Schart Hyman. (Holiday House, 1999)—Caldecott Honor, 2000.

Paul Brett Johnson—Fried Chicken

When I was growing up in the small Appalachian town of Mousie, Kentucky, it was pretty much accepted as fact that fried chicken was the favorite food of preachers—all preachers.

—Paul Brett Johnson

Paul Brett Johnson

Birthday: May 19

Favorite place: By a mountain spring in the summer

Favorite foods: BLT (bacon, lettuce, tomato) sandwich, pinto beans with corn bread, pizza, and of course, fried chicken

Family:

There are many special people in Johnson's life; his cat Carly thinks she's the most important family member.

Home:

Childhood—Mousie, Kentucky

Now—Lexington, Kentucky

Paul Brett Johnson was raised in Knott County, Kentucky, in a small town called Mousie. It wasn't named Mousie because it was so small but because it was named after the first postmaster's daughter—Mousie Martin. The town could have been named "Kitty" after Mousie's older sister. As a boy, Johnson wanted to be a basketball player. Unfortunately, he wasn't very good at it. He was good at drawing though, and even before he could write, he made a book— with pictures instead of words. His parents arranged for private lessons with art instructors at Alice Lloyd College. Later Johnson attended the University of Kentucky. A course in children's literature piqued his interest in children's books, but he had to make a living. After college he held several jobs including elementary school teacher and photographer. Eventually, though, he decided to open an art gallery, and he set up a studio-gallery in an abandoned garage. For twenty years Johnson made his living as an artist. Even though he had occasionally submitted a story to publishers, it wasn't until the early 1990s that Johnson began to really focus on children's books. In 1993, his first book, *The Cow Who Wouldn't Come Down* was published.

For the past thirty-five years Johnson has lived in an old downtown neighborhood in Lexington, Kentucky, in a big house with three porches. In the southern tradition porches and storytelling do seem to go together.

CORNBREAD AND ITS VARIATIONS

Native Americans made cornbread long before the first Europeans settled the Americas. The earliest cornbreads were called "pone," from the Algonquin word *apan,* and were a simple mixture of cornmeal, salt, and water. Recipes developed in most regions of the United States. Cornbread recipes differ much between the northern and southern states. When fried in a skillet, cornbread was sometimes called "Johnny cake" (perhaps a corruption of the term "journey cake") and taken by travelers on their journeys. Cornbreads made in the northern states are generally sweeter and more cake-like because of the greater amounts of sugar and flour used in the recipes. Southern cornbreads use little sugar or flour.

Appalachian Corn Bread

Cornbread was traditionally baked in an iron skillet and included bacon grease as an ingredient and to keep the bread from sticking to the pan.

Put 3 tablespoons bacon grease in a cast iron skillet and put into a 450° F oven to preheat.

Mix all dry ingredients together:

- 1 1/2 cups white cornmeal or 1 cup yellow (your preference)
- 1/2 cup flour (1 cup if using yellow cornmeal)
- 1 tablespoon baking powder
- 1/3 teaspoon baking soda (may omit if not using buttermilk)

In another bowl, mix together and add evenly to the dry ingredients:

- 1 1/3 cups buttermilk or sweet milk
- 1 large egg

When the oven has reached the full temperature remove skillet and pour hot bacon grease into the batter; mix well. Pour batter back into the skillet. (Batter should immediately begin to sizzle and should sear the outside of cornbread to keep it from sticking to the skillet.) Bake cornbread in the skillet for 10 to 15 minutes. Use a toothpick to test for doneness. When cornbread is done, remove skillet from oven, and immediately turn cornbread out of the skillet.

Old Drye Frye Chicken

- 1 frying chicken, cut into pieces

Add any of the following seasonings (or others of your choice) to one cup of flour:

- 2 teaspoons salt
- pepper to taste
- garlic powder
- onion powder

Mix seasonings and flour so spices are evenly distributed.

Roll chicken pieces in flour until covered and shake off excess flour.

Put enough oil in an iron skillet to make a depth of about a 1/2 inch. Heat until the oil is very hot (about 365° F) and spits when a drop of water hits it, or you can test by dropping a 2-inch square of bread into the oil. It should turn golden brown in 1 minute.

Use tongs or a long fork to gently place floured pieces of chicken into the frying skillet. Turn on each side until each piece is golden brown on all sides (about 7 minutes each side). Reduce heat to medium while you are cooking chicken. Once each side is golden brown, cover and continue cooking for 5 to 10 more minutes or remove from skillet and continue cooking in a 350° F oven. Total cooking time: 30 to 35 minutes, depending on the size of each piece of chicken.

Selected Books by Paul Brett Johnson

Bearhide and Crow. (Holiday House, 2000)

The Cow Who Wouldn't Come Down. (Orchard, 1993; Scholastic, 2002 pb)

Fearless Jack. (Margaret Elderry, 2001)

The Goose Who Went Off in a Huff. (Orchard, 2001)

Jack Outwits the Giants. (Margaret Elderry, 2002)

Little Bunny Foo Foo: Told and Sung by the Good Fairy. (Harcourt, 2004)

Mr. Persnickety and the Cat Lady. (Orchard 2000)

Old Dry Frye: A Deliciously Funny Tall Tale. (Scholastic, 2001)

More Books: Appalachian Settings

Birdseye, Tom. *Airmail to the Moon.* (Holiday House, 1988)

Chase, Richard. *Grandfather Tales.* (Houghton Mifflin, 2003; originally published in 1948)

Chase, Richard. *Jack Tales.* (Houghton Mifflin, 2003; originally published in 1943)

Gravelle, Karen. *Growing Up in a Holler in the Mountains: An Appalachian Childhood.* (Franklin Watts, 1997)

Haley, Gail. *Mountain Jack Tales.* (Parkway, 2002)

Lyon, George Ella. *Mama Is a Miner.* Illustrated by Peter Catalanotto. (Orchard, 1994)

Milnes, Gerald. *Granny Will Your Dog Bite and Other Mountain Rhymes.* Illustrated by Kimberly Bulcken Root. (August House Littlefolk, 1999)

Page, Linda Garland, and Hilton Smith. *Foxfire Book of Appalachian Toys and Games.* (University of North Carolina, 1993)

Rylant, Cynthia. *Appalachia: The Voices of Sleeping Birds.* Illustrated by Barry Moser. (Harcourt Brace, 1991)

Rylant, Cynthia. *The Relatives Came.* Illustrated by Stephen Gammell. (Bradbury, 1985)

Rylant, Cynthia. *Waiting to Waltz: A Childhood.* (Bradbury, 1984)

Rylant, Cynthia. *When I Was Young in the Mountains.* Illustrated by Diane Goode. (Dutton, 1982)

Rylant, Cynthia. *Silver Packages: An Appalachian Christmas Story.* Illustrated by Chris K. Soentpiet. (Orchard, 1997)

Keiko Kasza—Potato Salad

Keiko Kasza

Birthday: December 23
Favorite foods: Too many to name
Family:
    Spouse—Gregory
    Sons—Kosuki and Taisuke
Home:
    Childhood—Hiroshima, Japan
    Now—Bloomington, Indiana

Food plays a key role in my picture books. In My Lucky Day, a fox cooks a spaghetti dinner for a piglet. In A Mother for Choco, Mrs. Bear bakes an apple pie for her children. In The Wolf's Chicken Stew, a wolf cooks 100 pancakes, doughnuts, cookies for 100 little chicks.

—Keiko Kasza

If Keiko Kasza were not an author and illustrator, she might just be a restaurant chef. She is admittedly a "good cook" and has put food in several of her books. Food is important to her.

"I know what you are imagining. 'Keiko must think of food 24/7!' Well, it's true, I am crazy about food! But there is another reason why food comes up in my books constantly. Food is connected to many of the best, most vivid experiences of my life.

"I grew up in Japan, of course, so some of the food I love may seem rather strange to people from other countries. When I was a girl, my mother always prepared special food for our New Year's celebration. She would make a soup with rice cakes called *ozoni,* which was topped with a piece of salmon. Knowing that I loved salmon, she always put two pieces of fish in my soup. And when my brothers or I had a birthday, we could request any kind of dinner we wanted. I always chose to eat crab, because my birthday is in December, which is in the middle of crab season.

"Even during the hot, humid summer, when it is easy to lose one's appetite, my mother had the answer. She would make a dish called *hiyashi-somen,* in which noodles are served cold in ice water. My childhood was so rich in food that I sometimes wonder what kind of person I would be without my mother's wonderful cooking. It's natural for me to include food in my books for children.

"It is important for everyone to maintain traditions of food from generation to generation. Without spending a lot of money we can hand down a rich cultural heritage, one that is blessed with a love beyond measure."

—Keiko Kasza

Wolf's Chocolate Chip Cookies

Blend 5 cups oatmeal until it is very fine. Set aside.

Finely grate 2 chocolate bars—4–6 ounces each. Set aside.

Cream together:

- 2 cups butter
- 2 cups white sugar
- 2 cups brown sugar

Add:

- 4 eggs
- 2 teaspoons vanilla

To the creamed mixture add:

- 2 teaspoons baking soda
- 2 teaspoons salt
- 2 teaspoons baking powder
- 4 cups unbleached flour
- The blended oatmeal (5 cups)

Mix all dry ingredients into the creamed mixture.

Add in:

- 24 ounces (two 12-ounce bags) milk chocolate chips
- The grated chocolate bars (each 4–6 ounces)
- 3 cups chopped nuts (optional)

Bake as usual, at about 375° F for roughly 10 minutes depending on the size of your cookies. Makes 100 cookies.

My Mother's Potato Salad

- 5 potatoes, peeled and cut in half
- 1 cucumber, peeled and sliced very thin
- 1/2 small onion, sliced super thin
- 1 1/2 teaspoons of salt
- 2 tablespoons of sugar
- dash of white pepper
- 3 tablespoons of vinegar
- 1/2 cup of mayonnaise
- salt and pepper to taste

Boil the potatoes until tender. While they are boiling, sprinkle 1/2 teaspoon of salt on the cucumber and onion. When the potato is done, mush it with the sugar, one teaspoon of salt, and the white pepper and vinegar. After the sugar is dissolved, mix in the mayonnaise. Squeeze the cucumber and onion slices to take out any excess water, and mix in the potato. You can adjust the recipe to taste with more salt and pepper. My mother used to serve this as a side dish with fried shrimp.

Signature Recipe—Keiko Kasza

Selected Books Written/Illustrated by Keiko Kasza

Don't Laugh, Joe! (Putnam, 1997)

Dorothy and Mikey. (Putnam, 1999)

Grandpa Toad's Secrets. (Putnam, 1995)

The Mightiest. (Putnam, 2001)

Mother for Choco. (Putnam, 1992)

My Lucky Day. (Putnam, 2003)

The Pigs' Picnic. (Putnam, 1988)

Rat and the Tiger. (Putnam, 1993)

When The Elephant Walks. (Putnam, 1990)

The Wolf's Chicken Stew. (Putnam, 1987)

100 Days Tales

In many schools, the 100th day of school has become a day of celebration, and to put that focus on the number 100, students often read stories that feature that quantity. In Keiko Kasza's *The Wolf's Chicken Stew,* a wolf who wants to fatten up a hen for his stew pot, bakes goodies to take to her. Unbeknownst to him he is also feeding her 100 chicks when he leaves 100 pancakes, doughnuts, and cookies on the hen's doorstep. In addition to that title, here are some of our other favorites.

Cuyler, Margaret. *100th Day Worries.* Illustrated by Arthur Howard. (Simon & Schuster, 2000)

Frith, Michael K. *I'll Teach My Dog 100 Words.* Illustrated by P. D. Eastman. (Random House, 1973)

Giff, Patricia Reilly. *The 100 Book Race: Hog Wild in the Reading Room.* Illustrated by Blanche Sims. (Scholastic, 1997)

Harris, Trudy. *100 Days of School.* Illustrated by Beth Griffis Johnson. (Millbrook, 2000)

Mathis, Sharon Bell. *One Hundred Penny Box.* Illustrated by Leo and Diane Dillon. (Puffin, 1986)

Medearis, Angela Shelf. *The 100th Day of School.* Illustrated by Joan Holub. (Scholastic, 1996)

Pinczes, Eleanor. *One Hundred Hungry Ants.* Illustrated by Bonnie MacKain. (Houghton Mifflin, 1993)

Ryan, Pam Munoz. *One Hundred Is a Family.* Illustrated by Benrei Huang. (Hyperion, 1996)

Slate, Joseph. *Miss Bindergarten Celebrates the 100th Day of Kindergarten.* Illustrated by Ashley Wolff. (Dutton, 1998)

Smith, Mavis. *Fluffy's 100th Day at School.* (Scholastic, 2000)

Szekeres, Cyndy. *I Can Count 100 Bunnies and So Can You!* (Cartwheel, 1999)

Wells, Rosemary. *Emily's First 100 Days of School.* (Hyperion, 2000)

Steven Kellogg—Hot Marshmallow Cheesecake with Raspberry Fudge Sauce

"Hot marshmallow cheese cake with raspberry fudge sauce!" she announced. With those words Jenny the mouse ushers in the climax of her holiday banquet to celebrate National Rodent Day.

—from *Island of the Skog* by Steven Kellogg

Photo: Sharron L. McElmeel

Steven Kellogg grew up drawing and telling stories to his sisters Patti (Trish) and Martha. He loved drawing animals and birds. His interest continued through high school and on into his study at the Rhode Island School of Design. During his senior year, he studied in Italy, and upon his return he pursued graduate study at the American University in Washington, D.C., and instructed classes as well. During this time, Kellogg began to submit manuscripts to publishers, and he found a whole new set of young children to whom he could tell stories. He met his future wife, Helen Hill, and her six picture-book-age children: Pam, Melanie, Laurie, Kim, Kevin, and Colin. They moved to Connecticut to a vintage farmhouse where they raised the children and Kellogg created illustrations for his many books. This home is also where the real Pinkerton (the dog) and Second-hand Rose (the cat) lived. Eventually the children grew up, grandchildren began to inspire some of his books, and the Kelloggs moved 200 miles away to a farmstead near Essex, New York, where they have lived for several years. A yellow barn on the farmstead houses Kellogg's studio, where he continues to illustrate and write children's picture books.

Steven Kellogg

Birthday: October 26

Favorite place: The old yellow barn overlooking Lake Champlain in which my studio is located.

Favorite foods: pears, apples, and ice cream

Family:
  Spouse—Helen

Home:
  Childhood—Connecticut
  Now—Blockhouse Farm, Essex, New York

129

Waffle Irons in Kellogg's Books

In *The Island of the Skog,* Jenny and her friends gather around a waffle iron to keep warm. In Kellogg's version of *The Three Little Pigs,* Percy, Peter, and Prudence help their mother Serafina establish waffleries around the world. The wacky version of the traditional tale ends with Serafina reading to her dozens of grandchildren, her children operating and expanding the waffle business, and the wolf—having had the meanness seared out of him—relaxing on the beach in the Gulf of Pasta.

WAFFLE COOKIES

One way to expand a wafflery is to create a new product. A waffle cookie might be just the item Percy, Peter, and Prudence might want to test market. Here's a recipe for a version of a cookie that is named in their mother's honor.

Granny Serafina's Chocolate Waffle Cookies

Mix together until creamy:

- 2 cups sugar
- 1 cup (2 sticks) margarine
- 4 eggs

Add and beat until fully incorporated:

- 4 squares chocolate, melted
- 1 cup milk

Mix in:

- 3 cups flour
- 2 teaspoons baking powder
- 1/2 teaspoon salt

Drop by teaspoons onto hot waffle iron (set on medium) and bake just as you would a waffle. Put one teaspoon in each waffle section. While still warm sprinkle with powdered sugar or cool and frost with any favorite frosting. Baking takes about 1 minute. Makes 4 dozen.

Jenny's Hot Marshmallow Cheesecake with Raspberry Fudge Sauce

Prepare a graham-cracker crust:

- 1 1/2 cups graham-cracker crumbs
- 1 teaspoon ground cinnamon
- 3/4 cup granulated sugar
- 6 tablespoons butter, melted

Combine dry ingredients. Sprinkle butter over dry ingredients and toss lightly with a fork, until all crumbs are covered evenly. Press the crumb mixture into a buttered 10-inch springform pan. Cover the bottom of the pan and press the crumbs part way up the sides. Chill the crust in the freezer for 20 minutes, until set.

Illustration: Steven Kellogg

Preheat the oven to 400° F.

Prepare the cheesecake batter:

- 2 pounds cream cheese
- 1/2 cup granulated sugar
- 2 large eggs, lightly beaten
- 2 tablespoons cornstarch
- 1 cup sour cream

In a large mixing bowl, cream the cream cheese and sugar until light and fluffy. Beat in the eggs, vanilla, and cornstarch until just mixed. Stir in the sour cream until the batter is smooth. Pour the mixture into the prepared graham-cracker crust. Bake the cake for approximately 40 minutes, until the edges are raised and just starting to brown. Turn off the oven and let the cake cool with the door propped open, until room temperature. Slide a knife around the edge of the pan to loosen the cake. Chill for several hours.

Make raspberry fudge sauce:

- 4.5 ounces semisweet chocolate chips
- 6 tablespoons unsweetened cocoa
- 1 cup water
- 9 tablespoons unsalted butter
- 1/2 cup granulated sugar
- 1/2 cup seedless raspberry preserves, pureed until completely smooth.

Simmer and stir all ingredients in a small heavy sauce pan, until sugar has dissolved. Stop stirring and bring to a moderate boil for 5 to 10 minutes, until mixture thickens slightly. Swirl the mixture in the pan, but don't stir. Cool slightly and add 1 1/2 teaspoons vanilla. Serve warm.

(Continued)

Continued

Before serving:

Preheat the oven to broil. Top the cheesecake with 2 cups mini-marshmallows in an even layer. Broil until marshmallows are golden brown and puffy. Remove springform pan and cut the cheesecake with a hot knife.

To serve:

Pour 3 tablespoons of raspberry fudge sauce on a plate and place a piece of warm cheesecake in the center of the pool of sauce. Garnish with a few fresh raspberries. Serves 12.

Selected Books Written/Illustrated by Steven Kellogg

A-Hunting We Will Go! Retold by Steven Kellogg. (William Morrow, 1998)

Big Bear Ball. Text by Joanne Ryder. (HarperCollins, 2001)

Clorinda. Text by Robert Kinerk. (Simon & Schuster, 2002)

Clorinda the Fearless. Text by Robert Kinerk. (Simon & Schuster, 2005)

Give the Dog a Bone. Retold by Steven Kellogg. (SeaStar Books, 2000)

The Island of the Skog. (Dial, 1973)

Pinkerton Series (Dial): *Pinkerton, Behave*! (1979); *A Rose for Pinkerton* (1981); *Tallyho, Pinkerton*! (1982); *Prehistoric Pinkerton* (1987); *A Penguin Pup for Pinkerton* (2001)

The Three Little Pigs. Retold by Steven Kellogg. (William Morrow, 1997)

The Three Sillies. Retold by Steven Kellogg. (Candlewick Press, 1999)

Ready! Set! Measure! Climb Aboard! Text by David M. Schwartz. (HarperCollins, 2002)

Kellogg's watercolors often begin the story with illustrations on the end pages, half-title page, title page, and dedication page. Look for hidden bits of humor, and added details, in all of his illustrations. He creates imaginative titles to place on the spines of books shown in illustrations, signs on the wall—small bits of humor in any available part of the illustration.

Jane Kurtz—Orange Spirals

The first thing I ever baked by myself—in the wood stove—was Cowboy Coffee Cake. I found the recipe in a book the year my mom went to spend Christmas with my older sister, who was in boarding school in Egypt. When I served it for Christmas brunch, my family and the nurse and teacher who were our guests declared it delicious, and I felt great!

—Jane Kurtz

Jane Kurtz

Birthday: April 17

Favorite place: Maji, Ethiopia

Favorite foods: breads of all kinds, peaches, blueberries, fresh vegetables

Family:

Spouse—Leonard Goering

Son—David, Jonathan

Daughter—Rebekah

Home:

Childhood—Ethiopia

Now—Kansas

"In Ethiopia, where I spent most of my childhood, many people eat *wat* and *injera* every single day. The *wat* is a spicy stew that can be made with many different ingredients, including chicken, lamb, beef, lentils, and split peas. Most varieties of *wat* have plenty of onions and plenty of spice, including red pepper. When my brother was little, he would eat a bite of the *wat* and cry because it was so spicy hot—but he liked the taste, so he would take another bite and cry some more. *Injera* is like a very big, flexible pancake. It's made with teff grain, which isn't commonly used in the U.S., and the batter is allowed to sit for a few days until it becomes sour, just like sour dough starter. To eat in the traditional Ethiopian style, our family sat around one dish or basket full of food, tore off pieces of *injera* with our fingers, and scooped up the *wat*. My mother also brought recipes and favorite meals with her from the United States—and taught them to school boys who worked in our house to earn money so they could buy pencils, paper, and other supplies. One of the most wonderful things I remember eating was orange spirals, something my mom learned to make from my dad's mom. They tasted like cinnamon rolls, except that instead of cinnamon, the filling was made with grated orange peel mixed with sugar and butter. Oranges didn't grow near where I grew up, so this had to be a special treat."

—Jane Kurtz

THE HISTORY OF CAKE

In ancient times, the cakes were very different from what we know as cake today. The early cakes were more bread-like and sweetened with honey. Nuts and dried fruits were often added. According to the *Oxford English Dictionary,* the use of the word "cake" traces to the thirteenth century. It wasn't until the 1800s that cakes made with extra refined white flour and baking powder instead of yeast became prevalent.

This coffee cake recipe is from the 1940s—and very possibly might have been in a recipe book that Jane's mom would have taken with her when the family left the United States to become missionaries in Ethiopia.

Cowboy Coffee Cake

Combine until crumbly:

- 2 1/2 cups flour
- 2 cups brown sugar
- 1/2 teaspoon salt
- 2/3 cup shortening

Set aside 1/2 cup of crumbly mixture
(to sprinkle on top of cake)

To larger portion of crumbly mixture add:

- 2 teaspoons baking powder
- 1/2 teaspoon baking soda
- 1/2 teaspoon cinnamon
- 1/2 teaspoon nutmeg

Mix well and then add and stir until smooth:

- 1 cup sour milk
- 2 well-beaten eggs

Place batter in two 8-inch round or square baking pans. Sprinkle the top of each cake pan with half the reserved crumbly mixture. Optional: Sprinkle 1/2 teaspoon cinnamon and 1/2 cup chopped nuts over the crumbs.

Variation: Before sprinkling the crumbly topping on the batter spread 1 cup cherry, raspberry, or other pie filling, and then sprinkle the crumbly topping on top of the pie filling.

Bake at 375° F for 25 to 30 minutes.

Orange Spirals

- 1/2 cup warm milk
- 1/2 cup warm water
- 2 tablespoons dried yeast
- 1/4 cup butter
- 1/4 cup sugar
- 3/4 teaspoon salt
- 1 egg
- 3 1/2 to 4 cups of flour
- Grated peel of one orange
- 1/4 cup butter
- 1/4 cup brown sugar
- Walnuts (optional)
- Muffin tins

Melt the butter and lightly beat the egg with a fork. Dissolve the yeast in the water, which should be warm but not hot. Mix together the milk, sugar, salt, and butter. Add the yeast and beaten egg. Mix well. Add the flour gradually, adding only enough so the dough isn't sticky and can be handled. Knead the dough lightly. Put it in a greased bowl, cover with a damp dish towel, and let it stand in a warm place until it doubles in size (1 to 2 hours). Meanwhile, grate the peel from one orange. Melt 1/4 cup of butter and add the orange peel. Punch down the dough and roll it into a big rectangle about 1/4-inch thick. Spread the melted butter mixture over the rectangle, sprinkle it with the sugar, and place walnuts at intervals—as many as you like. Starting with the long side, roll the dough into a fat snake. Cut into pieces about 1/2 to 1 inch thick. (Each piece should fit in a muffin hole and fill it about 1/2 to 3/4 full.) Grease the muffin tin and put one roll in each hole. Cover the muffin tin with the damp towel and let it rise until the rolls reach the top of the tin (about an hour). Bake at 400° F for 20 to 25 minutes. Remove from tin and let cool on a wire rack.

Signature Recipe—Jane Kurtz

Selected Books by Jane Kurtz

Bicycle Madness. (Henry Holt, 2003)

The Feverbird's Claw. (Greenwillow, 2004)

In the Small, Small Night. (Amistad, 2005)

Johnny Appleseed. (Aladdin, 2004)

Memories of Sun: Stories of Africa and America. (Amistad, 2003)

Mister Bones: Dinosaur Hunter. (Aladdin, 2004)

The Oregon Trail: Chasing the Dream. (Aladdin, 2005)

Rain Romp: Stomping Away a Grouchy Day. (Greenwillow, 2002)

Saba: Under the Hyena's Foot. (Pleasant Company, 2003)

The Storyteller's Beads. (Gulliver, 1998)

Water Hole Waiting. With Christopher Kurtz. (Greenwillow, 2002)

Elaine Landau—Scalloped Corn

Remember the last time you bit into a hot buttery ear of corn?

—from *Corn* by Elaine Landau

Elaine Landau

Birthday: February 15

Favorite place: Boothbay Harbor, Maine

Favorite foods: Lobster stuffed with crabmeat, hot pecan pie with whipped cream, and corn on the cob

Family:

    Spouse—Norman Pearl

    Son—Michael Brent Pearl

Home:

    Childhood—Lakewood, New Jersey

    Now—Miami, Florida

Elaine Landau was born and raised in New Jersey, and after graduating from New York University in 1970 she began working on a community newspaper in New York and later became an editor at Simon & Schuster. It was during this time that she wrote her first book with coauthor Jesse Jackson. She continued to research and write about a variety of topics. After a couple of years she entered Pratt Institute and earned a graduate degree in library science and became a public library director, while continuing to write. Landau's writing is often cited as being well researched and written. She writes extensively for readers from the young reader to the teenage reader on myriad subjects. She has explored topics as wide ranging as teen spending and dating to gun control to dinosaurs and pets. She has written about UFOs and the Loch Ness Monster, explorers and deadly diseases. Her insatiable curiosity continues to provide seeds for many new books of nonfiction. She has created simple introductions to foods such as chocolate and ice cream, as well as books about corn and tomatoes—books filled with historical acts, legends, trivia, and recipes.

"I grew up on a farm on the outskirts of Lakewood, New Jersey. Though it was a poultry farm, my parents also grew some corn and tomatoes. Many summer evenings we enjoyed 'farm dinners,' consisting of the sweet corn and fresh ripe tomatoes that my sister and I picked that afternoon. I'll never forget how delicious that hot buttery corn tasted with those sliced tomatoes.

137

"I now live in a large city, but I haven't given up that wonderful taste treat. On summer nights, I often serve my family fresh corn with sliced tomatoes. It's a way of sharing a wonderful time in my childhood, with my own child."

—**Elaine Landau**

QUICK CORN FACTS:

An average ear of corn has 800 kernels in 16 rows.

A pound of corn consists of approximately 1,300 kernels.

Twice the amount of corn is grown in the United States than any other crop.

Over 55 percent of the corn grown in Iowa (the leading corn-producing state) is exported to foreign markets.

Corn is a major ingredient in many food items such as cereals, peanut butter, snack foods, and soft drinks.

More than half of all the corn grown in the United States is grown in Iowa, Illinois, Nebraska, and Minnesota.

Corn is produced on every continent of the world except Antarctica.

Corn Bread Casserole

Elaine Landau's memories of hot buttery corn and fresh tomatoes can't always be duplicated in seasons when these fresh foods are not available, but here is a recipe for a corn dish with tomatoes that is delicious.

Prepare and bake a batch of corn bread. While the corn bread is baking (or plan to use left-over or dried-out corn bread) combine the following:

- 2 cans cream-style corn
- 2 cans whole kernel corn, drained
- 1 large onion, chopped fine
- 1 small green pepper, chopped fine
- 1 small red pepper, chopped fine, or 1 small tomato finely diced (dried tomatoes may be substituted)
- 2/3 cup milk
- 1 egg, well beaten
- 1 cup corn bread crumbs
- 1/4 cup melted butter
- Salt and pepper to taste

Pour batter into a greased 9 x 9 x 2-inch casserole dish and bake in a 375° F oven for 40 minutes or until toothpick in center comes out clean.

Corn Salad

Combine and set aside:

- 4 cups of freshly cut corn, cooked (or two 12-ounce cans whole kernel corn, drained)
- 3/4 cup diced cucumbers
- 1/4 cup diced onion
- 2 small tomatoes, chopped

Blend together:

- 1/4 cup sour cream
- 2 tablespoons mayonnaise
- 1 tablespoon vinegar
- 1/2 teaspoon salt
- 1/4 teaspoon dry mustard
- 1/4 teaspoon celery salt

Add sour cream mixture to corn mixture. Toss gently to coat vegetables. Chill corn salad thoroughly. Serve chilled.

Booklist

Read about Corn

Aliki. *Corn Is Maize: The Gift of the Indians.* (HarperCollins, 1982)

Arnosky, Jim. *Raccoons and Ripe Corn.* (Lothrop Lee & Shepard, 1987)

Barth, Edna. *Turkeys, Pilgrims, and Indian Corn: The Story of the Thanksgiving Symbols.* Illustrated by Ursula Arndt. (Clarion, 2000; reissue)

Fussell, Betty Harper. *Story of Corn.* (NorthPointe Press, 1999)

Selected Books Written by Elaine Landau

Holiday series: *Independence Day: Birthday of the United States*; *Columbus Day: Celebrating a Famous Explorer*; *Thanksgiving Day: A Time to Be Thankful.* (Enslow, 2001); *St. Patrick's Day*; *Valentine's Day: Candy, Love, and Hearts*; *Veterans Day: Remembering Our War Heroes*; *Earth Day: Keeping Our Planet Clean*; *Mardi Gras: Music, Parades, and Costumes.* (Enslow, 2002)

Series about countries: *Canada*; *France*; *Dominican Republic*; *Egypt*; *Peru.* (Children's Press, 2000)

Series about structures: *Canals*; *Bridges*; *Tunnels*; *Skyscrapers.* (Children's Press, 2001)

A President's Work: A Look at the Executive Branch. (Lerner Books, 2003)

Chocolate: Savor the Flavor. (Rourke Press, 2001)

Corn. (Children's Press, 1999)

Friendly Foes: A Look at Political Parties. (Lerner Books, 2003)

Heroine of the Titanic: The Real Unsinkable Molly Brown. (Clarion Books, 2001)

Ice Cream: The Cold Creamy Treat. (Rourke Press, 2001)

John F. Kennedy, Jr. (Twenty First Century Books, 2000)

Pizza: The Pie That's Not a Dessert. (Rourke Press, 2000)

Popcorn! Illustrated by Brian Lies. (Charlesbridge, 2003)

Pretzels: One of the World's Oldest Snack Foods. (Rourke Press, 2001)

Slave Narratives: The Journey to Freedom. (Franklin Watts, 2001)

Tomatoes. (Children's Press, 1999)

Deborah Nourse Lattimore—Shrimp Santorini

When I worked on my book The Prince of the Golden Ox I noticed that, as in The Flame of Peace, I had an active volcano blowing up. My daughter was also working on a volcano project for school around that same time. It seemed to be a theme. So, I blew up a dinner resembling a volcano.

—Deborah Nourse Lattimore
(on the creation of Shrimp Santorini)

Deborah Nourse Lattimore

Birthday: May 16

Favorite place: the ocean, or on a beautiful bluff overlooking it

Favorite foods: crispy duck, sautéed asparagus, and vast quantities of ice cream

Family:
Son—Nicholas
Daughter—Isabel

Home:
Childhood—Beverly Hills, California
Now—Pacific Palisades/Malibu, California

From the time she was young, Deborah Nourse Lattimore was surrounded by art. Her home was filled with sculptures and paintings from many cultures. As a four-year-old, she drew on the wall behind a large Mexican tapestry. Deborah and her grandmother were very close and spent a lot of time together. They visited museums and viewed art from different perspectives—literally, as sometimes they would get down on their hands and knees to view a sculpture from another angle. Her grandmother often took her to gatherings where they could practice drawing flowers or animals. At the fair they drew the vegetables. At the Los Angeles County Museum, Deborah and her grandmother drew their own versions of the masterpieces on exhibit. During one visit the two of them viewed a display of fancy ball gowns from the eighteenth century. Naturally they wondered what was under the dresses. So they sketched what they thought eighteenth-century underwear looked like. Years later she satisfied that curiosity when she wrote and illustrated *I Wonder What's Under There?!—a Brief History of Underwear.*

Her grandmother also read to her—folklore and tales of ancient people. Deborah liked to write, too. As a teenager she worked to earn money for art supplies and she sometimes created art to sell, or in a few cases to barter for merchandise that she wanted.

Her interest in Aztec and Mayan mythology and history intensified during her college years. She learned more about ancient civilizations: Aztecs, Mayan, and cultures in Greece, Rome, and Egypt. She even learned how to translate hieroglyphics.

Lattimore teaches frequently at the University of California at Los Angeles and is on the faculty at the Art Center of Design in Pasadena. Since 1986, she has created more than thirty books. She also sketches seven days a week in her third-floor studio of her home.

Pine-Nut Couscous

Couscous is a species of pasta originating in North Africa. Rather than being in the form of noodles or extruded shapes, couscous is granular. The raw pieces are roughly the size of coarse sugar grains. It is cooked in a broth and seasoned with spices. Pine nut couscous can be seasoned with 1/2 onion gently sautéed in olive oil, 1/4 teaspoon cumin, and 1/4 teaspoon paprika and cooked for a further minute. Fluff the couscous with a fork, and add the rind of 1/2 an orange, a 1/2 cup pine-nut kernels, and chopped parsley to the onion mixture.

Santorini is the island identified as Atlantis (most often), and it has a huge caldera in the middle. This works in a chef's favor—because if your shrimp dish looks like a big caldera, you've accomplished the effect of an explosion! Hurrah!

—Deborah Nourse Lattimore

Retsina: Greek table wine normally flavored with pine resin. The purpose of the pine resin was originally to help preserve the wine.

Shrimp Santorini

- 2 pounds large prawns
- 1 large piece of feta cheese
- 2 large cans (16 ounces) whole Italian tomatoes
- Fresh basil, salt, pepper, a little sautéed garlic (1/2 head), and a few red pepper flakes (according to your taste)

Make a batch of nice pine nut couscous. (This is the base of the volcano.)

Grill the shrimp (after butterflying them).

Heat up the tomatoes in a saucepan with the basil, salt, pepper, and garlic.

Arrange: Couscous on the bottom of baking dish, then build up shrimps into a volcano shape, alternating with tomatoes.

Dice feta cheese and arrange pieces at top and around shrimps as artistically as you like.

Broil just a few minutes to give the whole ensemble a sort of burnt/toasted, exploded look.

Serve with a Greek salad and (for the adults) chilled retsina (a Greek wine).

Signature Recipe—Deborah Nourse Lattimore

Selected Books Written/Illustrated by Deborah Lattimore

The Child of Atlantis. Text by Robert San Souci. (Golden Books, 2002)

The Flame of Peace: A Tale of the Aztecs (HarperCollins, 1987)

Gittel's Hands. Text by Erica Silverman. (Bridgewater Books, 1996)

I Wonder What's Under There?!—a Brief History of Underwear. Paper engineering by David A. Carter. (Harcourt Brace, 1998)

Medusa. (HarperCollins, 2000)

The Prince and the Golden Axe: A Minoan Tale. (HarperCollins, 1988)

Sasha's Matrioska Dolls. Text by Jana Dillon. (Farrar, Straus & Giroux, 2002)

The Sailor Who Captured the Sea: And Other Celtic Tales. (HarperCollins, 2002)

The Winged Cat and Other Tales of Ancient Civilizations. (HarperTrophy, 2003; a collection of three tales)

Melinda Long—Bumblebee Stew

*Who, in their right mind, would eat any-
thing made from a bumblebee? ...
Springtime was when I first tasted bumblebee stew.*

—Melinda Long

Melinda Long's imagination fueled her own childhood adventures with her brother. She was Batgirl and Mark was Batman. Together they played characters on television, and she became a pirate—hiding treasures, special rocks, and jewels (including her mother's earrings). Melinda Long teaches eighth-grade students in Greenville, South Carolina. But just like in her childhood, Long still acts—she has appeared in a local community production of *Joseph and the Amazing Technicolor Dreamcoat*, and she tells stories and writes and is a member of the Greenville Storyteller's Guild.

Melinda Long

Birthday: September 3

Favorite place: home

Favorite foods: sweet potatoes, squash, fresh tomatoes, peanut butter pie, pizza!

Family:

Spouse—Thom Long

Son—Bryan (May 24, 1991)

Daughter— Cathy (December 23, 1987)

Home:

Childhood—Spartanburg/ Travelers Rest, South Carolina

Now—Greenville, South Carolina

Booklist

Selected Books Written by Melinda Long

How I Became a Pirate. Illustrated by David Shannon. (Harcourt, 2003)

Hiccup Snickup. Illustrated by Thor Wickstrom. (Simon & Schuster, 2001)

When Papa Snores. Illustrated by Holly Meade. (Simon & Schuster, 2000)

Peanut Butter Pie

Melinda Long doesn't really care for Bumblebee Stew, but she does love peanut butter pie. This dish is made in three layers: a graham cracker crust (layer 1), a thin layer of fudge (layer 2), and a cream cheese and peanut butter filling (layer 3).

Layer 1: Graham Cracker Crust

Combine the following and pat into a 9-inch pie pan:

- 1 1/4 cups graham cracker crumbs
- 1/4 cup sugar
- 1/3 cup melted butter or margarine

Chill.

Layer 2: Fudge Layer

In a 3-quart heavy saucepan, cook:

- 1 cup granulated sugar
- 2 ounces bittersweet chocolate
- 1/3 cup evaporated milk
- 1 tablespoon corn syrup

Cook to the softball stage. Remove from stove and stir in:

- 1 heaping teaspoon of peanut butter

Pour into pie shell and chill thoroughly before adding layer 3.

Layer 3: Filling

In a large mixing bowl, beat together until creamy:

- 8 ounces cream cheese
- 1/2 cup peanut butter
- 1 cup powdered sugar
- 1 teaspoon vanilla
- 1/2 cup milk

Fold in 2 cups of prepared whipped topping until well blended.

Put filling layer in pie shell on top of the fudge layer. Garnish with chocolate curls or grated chocolate chips or walnuts.

Chill thoroughly before serving.

TO TEST FOR SOFT BALL STAGE:

Use fresh cold water each time you test the candy. In about 1 cup of cold water, spoon about 1/2 teaspoon of hot candy. Use a spoon to push the candy to form a ball. Gently pick the formed ball up (if it will not form a ball, it is not done)—the soft ball will flatten slightly when removed from water.

Bumblebee Stew—A Story

Who, in their right mind, would eat anything made from a bumblebee? Well, I did, or at least that's what I thought I was eating. When I was about five or six years old, my family lived in Spartanburg, South Carolina. We were only a few miles away from my maternal grandparents' big, old, white farmhouse, so we visited there frequently. We often spent weekends there, and during the summer, we sometimes stayed all week long. I have year-round memories of that glorious place, but my most vivid memories seem to come from the springs and summers. Springtime was when I first tasted Bumblebee Stew.

Visiting Grandma and Grandpa Huskey was like taking a little vacation, every time we went. Of course, there were my grandparents: Grandma, sweet, frail, and quiet as a whisper; Grandpa, tall, strong, and teasing—always teasing.

Aunt Alice, Uncle Clyde, and my four cousins, all older than me, lived in the house with Grandma and Grandpa. There was no bathroom there until I was much older. We used the outhouse when we needed to go, and baths were taken in a big galvanized washtub. Water was pumped in from the well and heated. In the spring, the yard was flooded with bumblebees. I was afraid of them and ran screaming whenever one was near. One day while we played Kick-the-Can and went hiding all over the yard and in the barn loft, one of the little black and yellow rascals buzzed right in my face. I screeched and went crying to my cousins Jessie and Judy. They comforted me, but my boy cousins, Kenneth and David, saw an opportunity. "Don't worry," they told me, "we're gettin' rid of those bumblebees anyway."

I was intrigued. "How?"

"Mama's in there right now cookin' up a pot of Bumblebee Stew." Kenneth told me.

"That's right," David added. "We're havin' it for supper tonight."

I ran inside to find my aunt stirring a pot of milky-looking stuff filled with chunky, black things. Bumblebees! It was true. I ran out of the house without noticing the small empty oyster can on the counter.

Later that evening, we sat down to a bowl of Bumblebee Stew and crackers. My aunt didn't understand why I picked so at my food, and my cousins just wouldn't stop giggling. Finally, Judy couldn't take anymore and confessed to the prank. My aunt tried to fuss, but just laughed instead.

To this very day, whenever I see my cousins, the subject of Bumblebee Stew usually pops up.

—Melinda Long

In *How I Became a Pirate,* Jeremy Jacob along with Braid Beard and his crew enjoy all kinds of great food. They never mention oyster stew, but I wouldn't be surprised if they had some. After all, they are in the middle of a whole bunch of seafood! I'm not a big fan of anything containing oysters for obvious reasons, but if you're adventurous, give this stew recipe a try.

—Melinda Long

Bumblebee Stew (Oyster Stew)

In a heavy sauce pan cook 1 pint oysters (fresh-shucked, or canned). Cook until the edges of the oysters begin to curl.

Add:

- 1 quart milk
- 1/4 cup butter
- salt and black pepper (to taste)

Heat slowly, being careful to not boil. Serve immediately with fresh saltine crackers.

Signature Recipe—Melinda Long

Betsy Maestro—Sour Cream Cookies

Betsy Maestro

Birthday: January 5

Favorite place: Wherever my family is!

Favorite foods: seafood, Thai food, ginger ice cream

Family:

    Spouse—Giulio

    Son—Marco

    Daughter—Daniela

Home:

    Childhood—Brooklyn, New York

    Now—Old Lyme, Connecticut

During her growing up years in New York City, Betsy Maestro was surrounded with books. She grew to love reading and books. For eleven years, Maestro taught kindergarten and first grade in Connecticut. Her favorite time of the school day was the time she read books to her students. In 1975, she quit teaching and became a full-time writer, and, along with her husband, Giulio, they have created more than a hundred nonfiction books. Today the Maestros live in a converted cow barn overlooking a salt marsh that is the habitat for many water birds.

Booklist

Books Written by Betsy Maestro

How Do Apples Grow? Illustrated by Giulio Maestro. (HarperTrophy, 2003; reprint)

Liberty or Death: The American Revolution, 1763–1783. Illustrated by Giulio Maestro. (HarperCollins, 2004)

A More Perfect Union: The Story of Our Constitution. Illustrated by Giulio Maestro. (HarperTrophy, 2000; reprint)

The Story of Clocks and Calendars: Marking a Millennium. Illustrated by Giulio Maestro. (HarperCollins, 1999)

"My maternal grandmother fled Russia with her family around 1917. They were Jews escaping persecution and came to America, where they settled in the Lower East Side of New York City....

"I grew up eating lots of sour cream, which seemed to be part of many of my favorite dishes. Sour cream mixed with strawberries, peaches, or bananas was the best lunch ever! When my grandmother made her famous blintzes, we put sour cream on top before we ate them. Sour cream was essential, as the last ingredient to my grandmother's Russian borscht. Even my favorite goodies were made with sour cream—sour cream coffee cake and the best ever sour cream cookies."

—Betsy Maestro

WHAT IS RUSSIAN BORSCHT?

A classic Russian borscht is a rich beet and vegetable soup that is always served hot, usually at lunchtime. The Ukrainian version often includes chunks of beef. Borscht is garnished with *smetana* (sour cream) and dill weed.

Russian Borscht

In a large soup kettle or Dutch oven combine the following:

- 6 cups consommé (or beef stock)
- 1 cup tomato sauce
- 1 1/2 cups shredded cabbage
- 3/4 cup thinly sliced celery
- 3/4 cup shredded carrots
- 3/4 cup thinly sliced onions

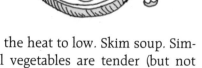

Bring the liquid to the boiling point and turn the heat to low. Skim soup. Simmer, covered for about 10 minutes or until vegetables are tender (but not mushy). Skim as needed.

Stir in:

- 1 teaspoon sugar
- 1 1/2 cups julienne strips of raw beets

Cover soup pot and simmer for 10 more minutes or until beets are tender. Salt and pepper to taste, if necessary. Stir in vinegar if you are using it. Turn soup into a tureen or individual soup bowls and sprinkle with dill weed. Add a dollop of sour cream to taste. Serve hot.

SOUR CREAM—WHAT IS IT?

Sour cream is used in many kitchens to make vegetable dips, thicken sauces, to top baked potatoes, and to garnish soups and salads. Used in baked goods, sour cream softens the product.

Cooks can make their own at home. Pasteurized cream lacks the bacteria that will allow the cream to sour. Instead, the cream will spoil. Adding 1 tablespoon of vinegar to 2 cups of unpasteurized cream will make the cream curdle if it is allowed to set out at room temperature for several hours.

If unpasteurized cream, is not available you can make another form of soured cream— créme fraîche; the taste is milder, but it may be an acceptable substitute for recipes that call for sour cream. You can make créme fraîche by adding 1 cup of buttermilk to 2 cups of heavy cream and leaving it out in a warm place (80° to 90° F; 26° to 32° C is ideal) for eight to twenty-four hours. Créme fraîche can be whipped.

Sour Cream Coffee Cake

Stir together in a bowl and blend until crumbly:
- 3 tablespoons margarine, softened
- 1/3 cup pecans, chopped
- 1/2 cup brown sugar

Set aside.

In large mixing bowl, beat the following together until smooth:
- 1 teaspoon vanilla
- 3/4 cup sugar
- 1/2 cup oil
- 3 eggs

Set aside.

In a separate bowl, mix:
- 2 cups flour
- 1 teaspoon baking powder
- 1 teaspoon baking soda
- 1/4 teaspoon salt

To the egg and sugar mixture, add the flour mixture, alternating with 1 cup of sour cream. Mix thoroughly after each addition. Layer batter and crumb mixture half at a time in greased tube pan. Bake at 350° F for 50 minutes or until a toothpick inserted in the coffee cake comes out clean.

Minnie Sherman's Sour Cream Cookies

- 1/4 cup butter
- 1 1/2 cups sugar
- 2 eggs
- 2 1/2 cups flour
- 1/4 teaspoon salt
- 1 teaspoon baking soda
- 1 cup sour cream
- 1 teaspoon nutmeg

Preheat oven to 375° F. Cream butter together with sugar. Add beaten eggs and blend well. Sift flour with salt and baking soda and add to creamed mixture. Add sour cream and nutmeg and mix well. Drop dough by tablespoons onto slightly greased cookie sheets and bake 12 to 15 minutes. Allow space between 1-inch pieces.

Signature Recipe—Betsy Maestro

Immigration

Betsy Maestro's grandparents immigrated from Russia to the United States in the early 1900s. Stories of other immigrants in a similar time are told in a multitude of books. These books might lead to a focus on a reader's own ancestors and their stories—and perhaps recipes they brought with them.

Bierman, Carol. *Journey to Ellis Island: How My Father Came to America.* (Madison Press Books, 1998; set in 1922)

Hesse, Karen. *Letters from Rifka.* (Henry Holt, 1992; a young Jewish girl's story of her family's immigration in 1919)

Lasky, Kathryn. *Dreams in the Golden Country: The Diary of Zipporah Feldman, a Jewish Immigrant Girl.* (Scholastic, 1998; set in the Lower East Side of New York in 1903–1904; a Jewish family in America)

Jacqueline Briggs Martin—Coconut Cake

Good Luck was a piece of Anna Mae Hill's coconut cake—sweet and crumbly and covered with cream whipped so thick fishermen said they could stand on it.

**—from *On Sand Island*
by Jacqueline Briggs Martin**

Jacqueline Briggs Martin

Birthday: April 15

Favorite place: Maine Meadow

Favorite foods: Homemade bread and soup

Family:

Spouse—Rich Martin

Son—Justin

Daughter—Sarah

Home:

Childhood—Maine

Now—Iowa

Jacqueline Briggs Martin grew up on a dairy farm near Turner, Maine. She walked through the meadow and the orchard with bountiful apple trees. Hugh, Jacqueline's father, loved working the land; her mother, Alice, was a full-time mother and farm bookkeeper. Jacqueline and her brothers and sisters often walked through the meadow and the orchard. Her mother was, according to Jacqueline, a wonderful cook and baker. One day she actually baked fifty pies in her kitchen. Apple trees and meadows show up in several of Jacqueline's books. The characters in her books are often industrious: *The Finest Horse in Town* is based on the lives of her two great aunts who ran a dry goods store; *Snowflake Bentley* focused on the persistence and hard work of Wilson A. Bentley; *The Lamp, the Ice, and the Boat Called the* Fish, told of the industrious Inupiak family that helped save the crew on the 1913 expedition in the Canadian Artic. *On Sand Island* came about when Martin spent part of one summer on Sand Island in the Apostle Islands of Lake Superior. In that book, a young boy, Carl, decides to build himself a boat; he also spends the summer picking strawberries, helping make fishnets, and trading other jobs for materials to make that boat. When the island residents celebrate the newest boat on the island, they come with fish stew made with butter and milk, warm bread and strawberry jam, and coconut cream cakes. Friends and neighbors ate and danced and sang their songs and looked toward a new day on Sand Island.

Jacqueline writes about her life and writing in *Jacqueline Briggs Martin and You* (Libraries Unlimited, 2005).

Strawberry Jam

Combine 2 cups strawberries, stemmed and crushed with 4 cups sugar in large bowl. Let set for 12 minutes and stir occasionally.

In a small saucepan, mix 3/4 cup water with 1 box of Sure-Jell and boil for 1 minute. Combine the strawberry and sugar mixture with Sure-Jell. Stir until sugar is dissolved. Pour strawberry jam into small jars. Refrigerate to use within a week or two. Freeze the remaining jars for use later.

Warm Bread

Mix: 1 1/2 packages dry yeast with 3/4 cup lukewarm water and 1/2 teaspoon sugar. Set aside.

Boil and mix: Boil 3 cups water and add 1 1/2 cups quick oats. Cook and stir for 1 minute.

Add to oat mixture: 2 tablespoons margarine, 1 tablespoon salt, 1/2 cup dark molasses. Stir until blended. Then:

In a large mixing bowl mix the oat/molasses mixture together with:

- 2 1/2 cups white or wheat bread flour
- 1/2 cup nonfat dry milk, and the dry yeast and water mixture. Beat for 4 minutes.

Add: Up to seven cups of white or wheat bread flour and knead the dough for 8 to 12 minutes—until the dough ball is smooth.

Let rise: allow the dough to double and then divide into three portions, knead each portion lightly into a loaf shape and place in greased bread pans. Let rise again until the loaves double in size.

Bake: 425° F for 10 minutes; reduce heat to 350° F. Bake another 35 to 45 minutes. Loaves should be brown and sound hollow when tapped on the bottom.

Cool on racks.

MORE BOOKS WITH A CONNECTION
TO COCONUT CAKE

On page 194 of the novel *I Stay Near You: One Story in Three* by M. E. Kerr (Harcourt, 1997), there is a three-layer coconut cake, and in Mem Fox's *Possum Magic* (Gulliver, 1990) Hush eats Lamington's—a traditional Australian food, which is sponge cake cut into squares and frosted with a thin chocolate frosting and rolled in coconut.

Coconut Cake

- 2 cups sugar
- 1/2 teaspoon salt
- 1 cup shortening
- 1 teaspoon vanilla
- 1 cup grated coconut
- 3 cups sifted all purpose flour
- 6 egg whites
- 2 teaspoons baking powder
- 1 cup evaporated milk
- 1/2 teaspoon black walnut flavoring

Mix: Sugar and shortening until fluffy. Add and mix in baking powder, salt, and milk. Gradually stir in flour. After mixing well, add black walnut flavoring and beaten egg whites and stir. Add 1 cup coconut. Put in a two 8-inch round layer pans or make cupcakes. Bake at 325° F for 40 to 45 minutes. Remove from oven when a toothpick is clean when it comes out of the center of the cake. While the cake is cooling, whip a half pint of sweet cream, add a teaspoon of vanilla, and beat until the cream is thick. Put whipped topping between layers and swirl on top and sides. Cut and serve.

Signature Recipe—Jacqueline Briggs Martin

Selected Books by Jacqueline Briggs Martin

Button, Bucket, Sky. Illustrated by Vicki Jo Redenbaugh. (Carolrhoda, 1998)

Higgins Bend Song and Dance. Illustrated by Brad Sneed. (Houghton Mifflin, 1997)

The Lamp, the Ice, and the Boat Called Fish. Illustrated by Beth Krommes. (Houghton Mifflin, 2000)

On Sand Island. Illustrated by David A. Johnson. (Houghton Mifflin, 2003)

Snowflake Bentley. Illustrated by Mary Azarian. (Houghton Mifflin, 1998; Caldecott Award, 1999)

Washing the Willow Tree Loon. Illustrated by Nancy Carpentar. (Simon & Schuster, 1995)

The Water Gift and the Pig of the Pig. Illustrated by Beth Krommes. (Houghton Mifflin, 2000)

Trading and Bartering

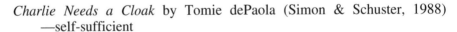

In *On Sand Island,* Carl barters his work for help with tasks that he is unable to do or for materials that he needs. Other titles can help build an understanding of the way our economic system developed from a society of self-sufficiency to a monetary system.

Charlie Needs a Cloak by Tomie dePaola (Simon & Schuster, 1988) —self-sufficient

The Goat in the Rug by Geraldine by Charles L. Blood and Martin Link. Illustrated by Nancy Winslow Parker. (Four Winds, 1980; Aladdin, 1990)—self-sufficient

A New Coat for Anna by Harriet Ziefert. Illustrated by Anita Lobel. (Knopf, 1986)—bartering goods for services

Pelle's New Suit by Elsa Beskow. (Gryphon House, 1993)—bartering services for services

Yuyi Morales—Tortillas

Photo: Tim O'Meara

"Just a minute, Señor Calavera," Grandma Beetle said. *"I will go with you right away, I have just THREE pounds of corn to make into tortillas."*
Señor Calavera rolled his eyes. He had to be very patient sometimes.
TRES. Three stacks of tortillas, counted Señor Calavera, and he put on his hat.

—**from *Just a Minute: A Trickster Tale and Counting Book* by Yuyi Morales**

Yuyi Morales

Birthday: November 7

Favorite place: The old streets of my hometown, Xalapa, in Mexico.

Favorite foods: Yogurt, quesadillas, and a Mexican goat milk candy called Cajeta.

Family: A big one with my two parents, two sisters, one brother, and many aunts, uncles and cousins.

Spouse—Tim O'Meara

Son—Kelly O'Meara (A passionate ten-year-old [in 2004] reader.)

Home:

Childhood—Xalapa, Mexico

Now—Pleasant Hill, California

Yuyi Morales's mother insisted that Yuyi learn to make tortillas when she was a child, just as her mother had learned from her own mother. Making tortillas is not as easy as it might look. Morales's mother told Yuri that when she (Yuyi's mother) was a child, women woke up early to grind the corn for the dough, in a stone called *metate*. Now most families buy their dough, and many even buy the tortillas from the tortilla factory. But Morales says, "There is nothing like a hand-made tortilla that you pat, pat, pat with the plump part of your palm.... I was never good at making tortillas." Yuyi says that when one did come out the right golden color, her mother would help her sprinkle it with salt and roll it into a *taquito*. The tortillas would be eaten with fresh cheese or with cilantro. Or sometimes they were broken into pieces and served with a plate of *frijoles* (beans).

Morales's cooking specialty is "the fat tortillas called *gorditas*." They are favorites of her husband, Tim, and her son, Kelly. Favorite toppings include beans, shredded onions, fresh cheese that they buy in San Francisco's Latino neighborhood, and a bit of fiery chile.

Basic Quesadillas

One of Yuyi Morales's favorite foods is quesadillas. They are relatively easy to make once you have the tortillas.

- 2 to 3 tablespoons oil, for frying
- 8 (8-inch) tortillas
- 2 cups Monterey Jack cheese

Place oil in an iron skillet over a medium heat. Once the oil is hot, place a tortilla into the skillet, then add a generous handful of cheese on top. Cook about 20 seconds to brown the bottom of tortilla. Fold one edge over the other and press edges down to make a covered half circle—a flat quesadilla. Cook another 20 seconds or so, then flip quesadilla. Cook a few more seconds. Cut into wedges and serve immediately with sour cream, salsa, or guacamole.

Use this basic quesadillas recipe to create the following variations.

Vegetable quesadilla: to the Monterey Jack cheese, add a few tablespoons of tomato and chopped onion.

Chicken quesadilla: to the Monterey Jack cheese, add a few tablespoons of cooked or shredded chicken breast.

Sausage or beef quesadilla: add a few tablespoons cooked, minced spicy sausage (such as chorizo) or cooked beef (hamburger or shredded beef).

Tortillas * Tortillas * Tortillas

Chavarria-Chairez, Becky. *Magda's Tortillas/Las tortillas de Magda*. Illustrated by Anne Vega. Translated by Julia Mercedes Castilla. (Arte Publico Press, 2000)

Kimmel, Eric A. *The Runaway Tortilla*. Illustrated by Randy Cecil. (Winslow, 2000)

Paulsen, Gary. *The Tortilla Factory*. Illustrated by Ruth Wright Paulsen. (Harcourt, 1995)

Tortillas

"Tortillas, hot off of the stove, soft and round in my hand, their smell always reminds me that they are full with the spirit of the corn.

"The ancient legend declares that, just like tortillas, we, Mexicans, are made of corn, shaped out of dough, and put to cook in the *comal* over the fire until we were done. But the legend also says that The Creator who made us took many attempts before he got us right.

"At first he shaped a man and put it to cook, but The Creator got distracted and left that man on the fire for too long, and his creation burned and came out black. So the creator took another ball of dough, shaped a second man, and put him to cook over the *comal* once more. Yet, worrying that his man might burn again, instead The Creator took him out the fire too soon, and the man came raw and white. A third time the creator tried, this time being very careful not too cook his man too much nor too little, and when he took him out of the fire, he saw that his creation was the golden color of toasted tortillas, and he was happy."

—Yuyi Morales

Tortillas

Corn tortillas are made with flour made from dried corn. The flour is called masa harina and is used for both tortillas and tamales. Masa harina can be found in many grocery stores but should be stored in an airtight container or in a freezer.

In a medium bowl, stir together and set aside:

- 1 1/2 cups masa harina
- 2 teaspoons salt

In a small saucepan over high heat, melt shortening in the water and bring to a boil:

- 2 teaspoons shortening
- 1 1/4 cups of water

Combine masa harina mixture with the water/shortening and blend well with a fork or pastry blender. Turn dough out on a floured board. Knead for 5 minutes.

Divide the dough into a dozen pieces and role each piece of dough into a 1-inch ball. Roll out each 1-inch ball to a paper-thin circle about 6 inches in diameter.

Use a large cast iron skillet. Heat very hot. Place a circle of dough into the hot skillet and cook until brown (about 30 seconds), turn and brown on the second side. Keep warm in a cloth towel until all tortillas are made.

Selected Books Written/Illustrated by Yuyi Morales

Harvesting Hope: The Story of Cesar Chavez. Text by Kathleen Krull. Illustrated by Yuyi Morales. (Harcourt, 2003)

Just a Minute: A Trickster Tale and Counting Book. Written and illustrated by Yuyi Morales. (Chronicle, 2003)

Sand Sister. Text by Amanda White. Illustrated by Yuyi Morales. (Barefoot Books, 2004)

Nancy Winslow Parker—Pound Cake

Photo: Dennis O'Grady

"The recipe used by the cook on Magellan's ships would, on a slim chance, be unearthed in the National Archives of Spain, a daunting task with uncertain results. We can only gasp at what people ate five hundred years ago, or even thirty years ago."

—Nancy Winslow Parker

Nancy Winslow Parker

Birthday: October 18

Favorite place: On the beach

Favorite foods: Deli type food

Home:

Childhood—Maplewood, New Jersey

Now—New York and New Jersey

Nancy Winslow Parker enjoys carpentry, tennis, gardening, and genealogy. She was raised in Maplewood, New Jersey, attended college in California where she earned an undergraduate degree in fine arts, and returned to the East Coast, where for more than twenty years she worked for large corporations in publicity and public relations departments. During this time, she studied the arts further, and in 1972, she decided to illustrate and write children's books on a full-time basis. After many rejections, she was successful in having her first book published in 1974. When a friend of hers was appointed to the president's cabinet, she got the idea to write *The President's Cabinet and How It Grew.* When she illustrated *Bugs,* she found that her long forgotten college class in biology was not so forgotten after all—she remembered more than she thought she would. Information learned in the course made the research for several of her information books much easier. Currently Nancy Winslow Parker divides her time between Mantoloking, New Jersey, and New York City.

"A very old book of mine was actually about how food took over my life for a spell. It was *Love from Aunt Betty* and was about a boy who received a recipe for a chocolate cake from his Aunt Betty. While writing the story and then illustrating it, I became involved in community work of my own invention—that of having a bake-off in the town and awarding ribbons to the winners of the categories–breads, cakes, pies, and cookies. Naturally, if you haven't guessed, it was the immersion in the writing and artwork that prompted me to get the town cooking, too. I did win a prize for the pound cake I submitted to the bake-off, but the recipe was not of my own invention, but from the Mills College Club of New York Cookbook.

"More recently, in a book I wrote and illustrated—*Land Ho! 50 Glorious Years in the Age of Exploration,* there is an endpaper devoted to the provisions for the men on board the ship that would take Magellan around the world in the fifteenth century. Not only did the crew have to survive the perilous voyage and cannibals, but perform their shipboard tasks on

sailor

a daily meal of onions, fish, and biscuits. The crew ate off of metal plates and was blessedly oblivious to bacteria. They had a personal spoon and drinking horn.

"In the hold of the ship were beans, lentils, chickpeas, biscuits, rice, cheeses, dried port, vinegar, honey, flour, mustard, figs, garlic and onions, and 3,200 pounds of raisins, currants, and onions—to last 230 men on five ships for two years.

[A recipe for the pound cake made by the ship's cook] has long gone to the graveyard of unhealthy desserts, as the cake is loaded with butter, sugar and eggs."

—Nancy Winslow Parker

Caramelized Onion Marmalade

Onions from the garden can be stored for months—this is a festive use for a surplus of onions. Peel and slice 2 to 3 sweet onions in half and then slice each half into 1/2-inch-wide half rings.

Sauté the onions in 3 tablespoons of butter in a large skillet, use medium heat. This will take about 1 minute. Toss and stir to evenly coat each onion piece.

Add:

onions

- 2 cups "double rich, double strength" canned beef broth, undiluted
- 2 tablespoons balsamic vinegar
- 2 teaspoons sugar
- 2 tablespoons parsley

Simmer for 15 minutes or more until the mixture thickens. Serve on grilled chicken, pork chops, or other meat, or put in a sterilized jar and refrigerate for use later.

Pound Cake

A great pound cake is rich and creamy and made now only for very special occasions because it is full of calories. A pound cake got its name from the fact that it used a pound of butter and a pound of sugar. This recipe might be very similar to the recipe for the pound cake that might have been included in the Mills College Club of New York Cookbook.

- Sift 3 cups of cake flour into a large mixing bowl.
- Add 1 pound of sugar and beat well.
- Add 1 pound of butter (you may melt to incorporate more easily).
- Add 6 large eggs and beat.

While continuing to beat, add:

- 2 teaspoons of pure vanilla extract
- 1/2 teaspoon salt
- 1/2 cup buttermilk

Beat until all lumps and air bubbles are removed from the mixture.

Pour the batter into a greased and floured standard tube cake pan. Bake the cake for 1 hour and 20 minutes in a preheated oven at 325° F.

Be careful not to check the cake too often because it will fall. Test with a toothpick or cake tester; when it comes out dry it is done.

Cool the cake and remove it from the pan. Frost with your favorite icing or sprinkle with confectioner's sugar.

Selected Books Written/Illustrated by Nancy Winslow Parker

Bugs. (Greenwillow, 1987)

Frogs, Toads, Lizards, and Salamanders. (Greenwillow, 1990)

Land Ho! 50 Glorious Years in the Age of Exploration. (HarperCollins, 2001)

Love from Aunt Betty. (Dodd, 1983)

Our Class Took a Trip to the Zoo. Text by Shirley Neitzel. (Greenwillow, 2002)

The President's Cabinet and How It Grew. (Parent's Magazine Press, 1978; revised edition, HarperCollins, 1991)

Who Will I Be?: A Halloween Rebus Story. Text by Shirley Neitzel. (Greenwillow, 2005)

John Paterson and Katherine Paterson
—Blueberry Muffins

Photo: Paterson Family Album. Used with permission of John and Katherine Paterson

The John & Katherine Paterson Family from the Paterson Family Album; photo used with the permission of John & Katherine Paterson.

The big man smiled. "Mmm, blueberries," he said. "You can taste one," said William, "but they're really for the queen."

—from *Blueberries for the Queen* by John and Katherine Paterson

Katherine Paterson, a twice-honored Newbery Award winner, first teamed with her husband, John, a Presbyterian minister to write a book with stories from the Old and New Testaments, *Images of God*, in 1998. Later the two collaborated on bringing an incident in John's life to young readers in picture book format when they created, *Blueberries for the Queen*. The story is set in 1942 and tells the story of William who takes blueberries to his Massachusetts neighbor—Queen Wilhelmina of the Netherlands. She and her family had fled there during the war years.

John Paterson

Birthday: November 11
Favorite place: home
Favorite foods: lamb chops
Family:
    Spouse—Katherine
    Sons—John Jr. and David
    Daughters—Lin and Mary
Home:
    Childhood—Middletown, Connecticut
    Now—Barre, Vermont

Katherine Paterson

Birthday: October 31
Favorite place: home
Favorite foods: Anything Chinese
Family:
    Spouse—John
    Sons—John Jr. and David
    Daughters—Lin and Mary
Home:
    Childhood—Huai'an, China
    Now—Barre, Vermont

Katherine's family had fled because of the war, too. In 1940, her family, missionaries in China, had to leave that country for good. Back in the United States, her family's moves took them to Virginia, North Carolina, West Virginia, and Tennessee. After teaching for a year and spending four years in Japan working to establish educational programs for a number of churches, she returned to the United States to attend the Union Seminary in New York City. That is where Katherine met and married John. Her first book was written for the Presbyterian church. Her first novels were about ancient Japan. *The Great Gilly Hopkins* came from her own experience as a foster parent, and *The Bridge to Terabithia* came from her son David's loss of a very good friend. Other books, some coauthored with John, rose from influences and incidents in their life: family, church, and community.

> "When John was nine, he learned that the Queen of the Netherlands, in exile because of World War II, was spending the summer of 1942 at the Lloyd Estate in Lee, Massachusetts. John's aunt and her family lived almost across the street, so when his family was going to visit the relatives, John picked a quart of blueberries from the field to take to the queen. The adults were patronizing, and his cousin hooted. He'd never be allowed to see the queen. Undaunted, John crossed the street with his blueberries. The guard sent him to the kitchen door. From there he was taken to the patio where he put his blueberries into the queen's own hands. She was very gracious. This incident became the basis for *Blueberries for the Queen*."
>
> **—Katherine Paterson**

Blueberry Pound Cake

Cream together:

- 1/2 cup butter or margarine   • 2 cups sugar   • 3 eggs

Then add and stir thoroughly:

- 1 cup milk

Add:

- 3 cups flour   • 1 teaspoon baking powder
- A dash of salt   • 1 teaspoon vanilla

Beat thoroughly and then fold in gently:

- 2 1/2 cups blueberries

Pour batter into a greased and floured 9 x 13–inch pan and bake in a preheated 350° F oven for about 50 to 60 minutes.

QUEEN WILHELMINA IN AMERICA

Queen Wilhelmina was the ruler of the Netherlands in 1940 when the Nazi soldiers invaded the country. She and her family fled to London, England, and set up a government-in-exile. During the summer of 1942, Queen Wilhelmina, her daughter Julianne (who later became queen), and her granddaughters—Julianne's young daughters, Beatrix (four and a half years old) and Irene (three years old) came to Massachusetts to spend a few of the summer months on the John Bross Lloyd estate just outside of Lee, Massachusetts. The estate was near the home of Paterson's aunt and uncle.

Blueberry Muffins

Combine and set aside:

- 1 egg, beaten
- 1/2 cup milk
- 1/4 cup melted shortening or oil

Sift together:

- 1 1/2 cups flour
- 1/2 cup sugar
- 2 teaspoons baking powder
- 1/2 teaspoons salt

Combine milk and egg mixture with flour mixture; mix lightly. There will be lumps.

Put in 1 cup blueberries, well-drained.

Combine just enough so the blueberries are evenly distributed.

Put in muffin tins, bake in a moderate oven (350°) for 20 to 25 minutes

Signature Recipe—Katherine Paterson

Selected Books Written by John Paterson and Katherine Paterson

Blueberries for the Queen. Illustrated by Susan Jeffers. (HarperCollins, 2004; picture book)

Consider the Lilies: Flowers of the Bible. Illustrated by Ann Ophelia Dowden. (Crowell, 1986; informational)

Images of God: Views of the Invisible. Illustrated by Alexander Koshkin. (Clarion, 1998; informational)

Selected Books Written by Katherine Paterson

Bridge to Terabithia. Illustrated by Donna Diamond. (Crowell, 1977)

Jacob Have I Loved. (Crowell, 1980)

Marvin One Too Many. Illustrated by Jane Clark Brown. (HarperCollins, 2001)

The Wide-Awake Princess. Illustrated by Vladimir Vagin. (Clarion, 2001)

World War II: The Dutch Experience and Others.

Adler, David A. *Hiding from the Nazis.* Illustrated by Karen Ritz. (Holiday House, 2001; a fictionalized account of the real Lore Baer, who was left with a Christian family to hide from the Nazis when the Germans invaded Holland)

Adler, David A. *One Yellow Daffodil: A Hanukkah Story.* Illustrated by Lloyd Bloom. (Gulliver Books/Harcourt Brace, 1995; a Holocaust survivor is reintroduced to his childhood traditions)

Oppenheim, Shulamith Levey. *The Lily Cupboard: A Story of the Holocaust.* Illustrated by Ronald Himler. (Charlotte Zolotow, 1992; a young girl, in Holland, hides in a cupboard to avoid detection by the Nazis)

Polacco, Patricia. *The Butterfly.* (Philomel, 2000; based on the true story of the author's aunt Monique and Monique's mother, Marcel Sollilage who was part of the French resistance during World War II)

Photo: Sharron L. McElmeel

Speaking of a supper of turnip greens, buttered cornbread, and a tall glass of buttermilk; and chess pie for dessert, all prepared by her mother, Reeves says, "To me, those meals were ambrosia; so simple and delicious—my mother, so relaxed and reminiscing, that I cannot think of a more fulfilling pairing than cornbread and chess pie."

—Jeni Reeves

Jeni Reeves

Birthday: May 16

Favorite place: Heartland Point in Cornwall, England

Favorite foods: Pecan and chess pie, meatloaf, Chateaubriand, and fiery hot vindaloo on a bed of basmati rice.

Family: Family of three in Cedar Rapids (well, now, two empty-nester parents); my late parents from upstate New York and Tennessee; my husband's family from Hampshire, England.

Spouse—Stuart Reeves, Ph.D., a research scientist.

Daughter—Tegan Reeves

Home:

Childhood—Geneva and Ithaca, New York

Now—Cedar Rapids, Iowa

Jeni Reeves was born in upstate New York, and studied art and sculpture in Italy. She was a television weather reporter in New York State, worked as a graphic designer in New York and London, painted landscapes and portraits in Africa, England, and America, and has exhibited her fine art in places such as Nairobi, New York, and Cedar Rapids, Iowa where she now lives and works. As a child, she often adapted and illustrated traditional stories. For several years, she and her husband, Stuart, lived in Kenya where Stuart worked as a scientist and their daughter Tegan was born. In 1998, Jeni began illustrating nonfiction picture books.

Reeves's mother often made this cornbread as a main ingredient for the family's Thanksgiving turkey stuffing. She says, "My mother made this into a single 'cake' in a round cast-iron skillet but this can also be made into a batter and spread on a griddle where it is called 'corn pone.'"

Skillet Cornbread

Dice three rashers of bacon and fry until crisp. Mix this with:

- 1 1/2 cups yellow cornmeal
- 1/2 cup plain flour
- 1 teaspoon baking powder
- 1 teaspoon salt
- 1/8 teaspoon sugar
- Beat 1 large egg into 3/4 cup buttermilk.

Add a little boiling water, one grated shallot (scallion or green onion), and 1/4 teaspoon of baking soda to the wet mixture.

Heat 2 tablespoons bacon grease or shortening in skillet, mix dry and wet ingredients together and pour into skillet. Bake in oven for 20 minutes at 350° F. Cool, slice, and butter.

Signature Recipe—Jeni Reeves

Cornbread and Chess Pie

"My mother, born and bred a Dixie chick, could not, would not, boil an egg until she married a Yankee ham from Upstate New York. In foreign territory, over time and hot ovens, she managed to conjure food from abracadabra to zbaglione. But when she was feeling homesick, she would hunker down over a cast-iron skillet for a bit of southern comfort: a supper of turnip greens, buttered cornbread, and a tall glass of buttermilk. If she was particularly nostalgic, dessert would follow with a hospitable slice of chess pie.

"I felt especially close to my mother and her southern roots when researching Candice Ransom's Virginian story of *Willie McLean and the Civil War Surrender*. Virginia is home, after all, to the first English mention of 'corn' as an Indian staple when Pocahontas offered it to the Jamestown colonists in 1607.

"The Confederate Army, especially, depended on cornmeal—both white and yellow—to make their 'hoe cakes.' In the spring of 1865, however, their rations had been captured; the remnants of Lee's army were close to starvation. The 'straggler' that Willie and

Lula met by the road was a desperate and hungry soldier. Willie, well fed, from a well-to-do merchant-class family did not understand hunger. After all, his father, Wilmer McLean, speculated in cane sugar. He had enough confederate money to keep the family in plenty of cornmeal, sugar, and vinegar: three ingredients used for another Virginian concoction, chess pie. Prior to the Civil War chess pie could be quite elaborate and rich. Many versions exist, one even named after Confederate President Jefferson Davis. My mother's chess pie is much more humble. I would speculate that the McLean household would become familiar with this version during the Reconstruction period after the war. A touch of sweetness amid much bitterness."

—Jeni Reeves

Mama's Chess Pie

For the pastry:

- 1 1/2 cups plain flour
- 1/4 teaspoon salt
- 2 tablespoons plus 1 teaspoon shortening
- 6 tablespoons of chopped, cold butter
- 4 to 5 tablespoons of cold water

Work the butter or shortening into the dry ingredients with a pastry cutter or cold fingers until the mixture has the consistency of fine breadcrumbs. Add cold water to make smooth, unsticky dough. Roll out on board to fit a 9-inch pie plate. Trim edges and chill while making the filling.

For the filling:

- 3 cups sugar
- 6 eggs
- 6 tablespoons white cornmeal
- 2 1/4 tablespoons vinegar
- 1 1/2 cups melted butter
- 2 teaspoons vanilla
- 1 teaspoon nutmeg
- 7 1/2 tablespoons of scalded milk

Illustration: Jeni Reeves

Mix all ingredients (except scalded milk) in a bowl. (Use a food processor if available.) Beat with a wire whisk for 3–5 minutes. Gradually add the warm milk and continue to beat. Pour into a chilled unbaked pie shell and bake at 350° F for 40 to 50 minutes.

Signature Recipe—Jeni Reeves

Selected Books Illustrated by Jeni Reeves

Babe Didrikson Zaharias: All-Around Athlete. Text by Jane Sutcliffe. (Lerner/Carolrhoda, 2000)

Booker T. Washington. Text by Thomas Amper. (Lerner/Carolrhoda, 1998)

Colors of Kenya. Text by Fran Sammis. (Lerner/Carolrhoda, 1998)

Colors of Russia. Text by Shannon Zemlicka. (Lerner/Carolrhoda, 2002)

Girl Who Struck Out Babe Ruth. Text by Jean L. S. Patrick. (Lerner/Carolrhoda, 2000)

Pocahontas. Text by Shannon Zemlicka. (Lerner/Carolrhoda, 2002)

Ramadan. Text by Susan Douglass. (Lerner/Carolrhoda, 2004)

Voice of Freedom: A Story about Frederick Douglass. Text by Maryann N. Weidt. (Lerner/Carolrhoda, 2001)

Willie McLean and the Civil War Surrender. Text by Candice Ransom. (Lerner/Carolrhoda, 2005)

Bread of All Kinds

Many cultures and ethnic groups bake bread, although each has its own variety and flavor. Cornbread as a southern favorite is included in *Everybody Bakes Bread* by Norah Dooley. Illustrated by Peter J. Thornton (Carolrhoda, 1995). Other books about bread include the following:

dePaola, Tomie. *Tony's Bread: An Italian Folktale.* (Putnam, 1996, reprint)

Gershator, David. *Bread Is for Eating* (Foods of the World). Henry Holt, 1998)

Morris, Ann. *Bread, Bread, Bread.* (HarperCollins, 1989)

Dian Curtis Regan—Brownies

"Publishing Liver Cookies, with its unappetizing recipes, like Okra Fudge and Tuna Shakes, taught me a lesson. Many school visits included a plate of liver cookies for the author. Yes, I invented them, but I wasn't prepared to eat them as long as the book was in print!"

—*Dian Curtis Regan*

Dian Curtis Regan

Birthday: May 17

Favorite place: Colorado

Favorite foods: Chocolate pudding and Mom's pot roast (but not together)

Family:

Spouse—John

Home:

Childhood—Colorado Springs, Colorado

Now—Kansas

Dian Regan was always interested in writing —it was one of her favorite subjects in school. After graduating from high school, she did some freelance writing, but her daytime job was as an inspector at Hewlett Packard; later she worked as a clerk at the gas company in Colorado Springs, Colorado. After attending a writer's conference, she decided to enroll at the University of Colorado at Boulder. By 1980, she had earned her degree in education, and she had met and married her husband, John. After working for a couple years as an elementary school teacher she decided to concentrate on being a full-time writer. She achieved such a success, she never did return to teaching. She's lived in Colorado, Texas, Oklahoma, Venezuela, and Kansas. During the three years Regan lived in Amarillo, Texas, she "met a wonderful group of children's writers, who came together to form a critique group." After moving away she was invited back to speak at a conference. Her fellow Texas writers hosted a reception for her and when she arrived she "was amazed to see a table decorated with my books, along with an amazing spread of food—and each dish had something to do with one of my books."

Texas Writers' Potluck Menu

Botswana Brownies (from *Monster of the Month Club*; Henry Holt, 1994)

Shipwreck Casserole and Liver Cookies (from *Liver Cookies*; Scholastic, 1991)

Peppermint candies (from *The Peppermint Race*; Henry Holt, 1994)

Granola (from *Monsters in the Attic*; Henry Holt, 1995)

Trail food (from *Game of Survival*; Avon, 1989)

Gummi Bears (from *I've Got Your Number*; Avon, 1986)

Coke and pretzels (from *The Perfect Age*; Avon, 1987)

Police cookies, cupcakes, and punch (from *Class with the Summer Birthdays*; Henry Holt, 1991)

Spaghetti (from *The Kissing Contest*; Scholastic, 1990)

Pizza (from *Princess Nevermore*; Scholastic, 1997)

A "cherry-flavored treat" (from *My Zombie Valentine*; Scholastic, 1993)

Many of these books are not available for purchase but can be located in school and public libraries. Search some of Regan's more recent titles and add some of your own menu items.

Left to right: Chery Webster, Ivon Cecil, Pat Willis, Beverly Hanlon,
Dia Hunter, Dian Curtis Regan, and Rosalyn Wolfe.

Never Enough Chocolate

With Dian Curtis Regan submitting a chocolate brownie recipe and declaring chocolate pudding as one of her favorite foods, we cannot help but think that she is a closet chocoholic. Here are some books that feature enough chocolate for all those who share her love of chocolate.

Burford, Betty. *Chocolate by Hershey: A Story about Milton S. Hershey* (a Carolrhoda Creative Minds Book). Illustrated by Loren Chantland. (CarolRhoda, 1994)

Burleigh, Robert. *Chocolate: Riches from the Rainforest.* (Abrams, 2002)

Catling, Patrick Skene. *The Chocolate Touch.* (Yearling, 1996)

Dahl, Roald. *Charlie and the Chocolate Factory.* (Knopf, 2001, revised)

Gwynne, Fred. *A Chocolate Moose for Dinner.* (Aladdin, 1988)

Kimmel, Robert. *Chocolate Fever.* (Yearling, 1978)

Rey, H.A. *Curious George Goes to a Chocolate Factory.* (Houghton Mifflin, 1998)

Snyder, Inez. *Beans to Chocolate* (Welcome Books: How Things Are Made). (Children's Press, 2003)

Woods, Samuel G. *Chocolate: From Start to Finish.* (Blackbirch, 1999)

Chocolate Lover's No Bake Cookies

Put in a saucepan and bring to rolling boil:

- 1 stick margarine
- 1/2 cup milk
- 2 cups sugar

Boil for 1 minute and then add:

- 1 cup chocolate chips
- 3 cups oatmeal
- 1 teaspoon vanilla extract

Stir well. Use a tablespoon to drop cookie clumps onto waxed paper.

BROWNIES—A FAMILY FAVORITE

Brownies show up in *Liver Cookies* and in Regan's books about monsters. Regan says that this recipe (*Curtis Brownies*) "is actually an old Curtis family recipe from the 1940s, and they are the best brownies in the world. The thicker the frosting, the better."

Curtis Brownies

- 1 stick butter
- 2 squares unsweetened chocolate
- 3 eggs
- 1 1/2 cups sugar
- 1 cup white flour
- dash salt
- 1 teaspoon vanilla
- 1 teaspoon cinnamon
- 1/4 cup chopped pecans

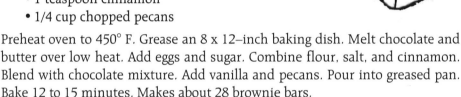

Preheat oven to 450° F. Grease an 8 x 12–inch baking dish. Melt chocolate and butter over low heat. Add eggs and sugar. Combine flour, salt, and cinnamon. Blend with chocolate mixture. Add vanilla and pecans. Pour into greased pan. Bake 12 to 15 minutes. Makes about 28 brownie bars.

Frosting:

- 2 cups powdered sugar
- 1/4 cup milk
- 1 1/2 squares unsweetened chocolate
- 1/4 stick butter

Melt chocolate and butter over low heat. Combine sugar and milk. Add to chocolate mixture. Beat until smooth and creamy. Frost brownies.

Signature Recipe—Dian Curtis Regan

 **Booklist**

Selected Books Written by Dian Curtis Regan

Chance. Illustrated by Dee Huxley. (Philomel, 2003)

Eight Nights of Chanukah Lights. Illustrated by Dawn Apperley. (Little Simon, 2002)

How Do You Know It's Halloween? Illustrated by Fumi Kosaka. (Little Simon, 2002)

A Sparkly Christmas Eve. Illustrated by Dawn Apperley. (Little Simon, 2002)

How Do You Know It's Easter? Illustrated by Fumi Kosaka. (Little Simon, 2004)

Barbara Santucci—Zucchini Bread

Photo: Jeff Swanberg

> *"Soon a new friend filled every chair. They ate zucchini cake, sipped lemonade, and played charades until the stars came out."*
>
> —from *Abby's Chairs*
> by Barbara Santucci

Barbara Santucci

Birthday: April 11

Favorite place: The woods and home

Favorite foods: Fruit and chocolate

Family:

    Spouse—Michael

    Daughters—Beth and Laura

Home:

    Childhood—Illinois

    Now—Rockford, Illinois

Barbara Santucci is a fine artist and an author of children books. After receiving an undergraduate degree from Loyola University in Chicago, she taught elementary and preschool and also worked as a librarian. She studied art at Rockford College and Northern Illinois University and works as a fine artist. Barbara divides her time between writing, painting, and teaching. She has received the Blanche Ellis Star, Leader in the Arts Award, 2001. She was selected as one of fifty artists to tour with the Illinois Women in the Arts Millennium Show. Her writing career came about as her love for children's literature inspired her to write for children. Her first books were published in 2002.

"When I moved to Iron Mountain, Michigan, as a young wife and mother, I planted my first garden. My baby daughter grew and my garden grew. Soon the zucchini plants took over and neighbors game me recipes for zucchini bread and cake. Now a new passion began—baking!

"When I wrote *Abby's Chairs* about Abby adjusting to her new move, it reminded me of my own move to Iron Mountain from Chicago away from family and friends. I thought it would be fun if her new friends came and one of them brought a zucchini cake to share.

"I still love to bake zucchini bread, although I no longer have a vegetable garden. But I love it when neighbors and friends offer me zucchini and love to share my bread with them."

—**Barbara Santucci**

177

Chocolate Zucchini Cake

Sift together and set aside:

- 2 cups all-purpose flour
- 1 teaspoon baking powder
- 1 teaspoon baking soda
- 1/4 teaspoon salt
- 1 teaspoon cinnamon
- 1/4 cup unsweetened cocoa

In a large mixing bowl beat until light in color and fluffy:

- 3 eggs

Then gradually beat in until fluffy:

- 1 1/2 cups granulated sugar

Beat in:

- 1/2 cup vegetable oil

Then alternately add (in three parts):

- flour mixture
- 3/4 cup buttermilk
- Fold into the batter
- 1/2 pound raw zucchini, shredded and drained
- 1 teaspoon vanilla extract
- 1 cup coarsely chopped pecans

Spoon batter into a greased and floured 10-inch Bundt pan.

Bake in a preheated 350° F oven for 55 to 60 minutes or until a wooden pick or cake tester comes out clean.

Cool and frost or sprinkle confectioner's sugar over the top.

Zucchini, Sautéed with Lemon

Trim the ends off six small zucchini and cut into 1/8-inch slices.

Heat 2 tablespoons olive oil over medium heat in a sauté skillet.

Add zucchini to the skillet.

Add a dash of salt and a dash of black pepper.

Cook, tossing and shaking until the zucchini begins to take color.

Add 1/8 teaspoon red pepper flakes and 2 tablespoons lemon juice.

Cover skillet and cook for approximately 2 minutes more. Do not over cook.

Remove from skillet and place on serving plate or in a bowl. Garnish with 2 tablespoons finely chopped parsley. Serve hot.

ZUCCHINI: WHAT IS IT?

Squash and pumpkin (or *cucurbita*) is a family of vegetables that includes the zucchini variety of squash. Zucchini is one of the best-known varieties of squash and one that is often the subject of jokes because of its ability to produce prolifically. Just a few plants will yield plenty for family, neighbors, and friends. Zucchini also cross-breeds with other members of the cucurbita family, including pumpkins. If you save the seed from one year to the next, it would not be unusual for a mutation to be produced in future crops.

Zucchini Bread

Combine and set aside:

- 2 cups flour
- 3 teaspoons cinnamon
- 2 teaspoons baking soda
- 1/2 teaspoon baking powder
- 1 teaspoon salt

Beat:

- 3 eggs
- 2 cups sugar
- 1 cup oil
- 2 teaspoons vanilla

Then add:

- 2 cups shredded zucchini (drained)

Mix well and then add flour mixture and 1 cup chopped walnuts.

After batter is thoroughly mixed pour into 8 1/2 x 4 1/2–inch bread pans.

Bake 35 minutes to 1 hour at 350° F.

Signature Recipe—Barbara Santucci

Selected Books Written by Barbara Santucci

Abby's Chairs. Illustrated by Debrah Santini. (Eerdmans Books, 2004)

Anna's Corn. Illustrated by Lloyd Bloom. (Eerdmans Books, 2002)

Loon Summer. Illustrated by Andrea Shine. (Eerdmans Books, 2002)

Photo: Michael Santucci

Q. What Do These Books Have in Common? (A. Zucchini.)

Creech, Sharon. *Walk Two Moons*. (HarperCollins, 1994). (p. 30)

Grover, Max. *The Accidental Zucchini: An Unexpected Alphabet.* (Voyager, 1997; reprint) (frontmatter).

Haddix, Margaret Peterson. *Among the Hidden*. (Simon & Schuster, 1998) (p. 150)

Howe, Deborah and James Howe. *Bunnicula: A Rabbit-Tale of Mystery*. (Atheneum, 1979). (p. 52)

Naylor, Phyllis. *Shiloh*. (Atheneum, 1991) (p. 28)

Snicket, Lemony. *The Slippery Slope* (A Series of Unfortunate Events, Book 10). (HarperCollins, 2003) (p. 8)

Spinelli, Jerry. *Maniac Magee*. (Little, Brown, 1990) (p. 87)

Tolan, Stephanie S. *Surviving the Applewhites*. (HarperCollins, 2002) (p. 63)

April Pulley Sayre—Pasta

One night after we ate pasta for dinner, I asked my family what book I should write next. One of them said, jokingly, "I think you should write about a guy named Al dente." Al dente is an Italian term that means "to the tooth," which is how you should cook pasta.

—April Pulley Sayre

April Pulley Sayre

Birthday: April 11

Favorite place: Panama

Favorite foods: blueberries, chocolate, and North Indian food

Family:

Spouse—Jeff (and seven pasta-eating nieces and nephews)

Home:

Childhood—Greenville, South Carolina

Now—South Bend, Indiana

April Pulley Sayre's interest in the out-of-doors came long before she became a published writer. During her childhood in South Carolina, she often picked flowers and watched insects and birds. She also read books and wrote—all things she has continued to do as an adult. After graduating from Duke University in 1987 she worked for a number of nature magazines including: National Geographical Society and the National Wildlife Federation. In 1991, she turned her full attention to being an author and sometime video producer. Traveling has become a means of seeking a story to tell. She and her husband, Jeff, also a writer, have tramped through swamps, wetlands, the rain forest; they once spent a month in Madagascar studying lemurs, scuba diving, and snorkeling over coral reefs. Most of the books are related to nature and animals in some way. One notable exception is *Noodle Man: The Pasta Superhero*. That story came right from her family dinner table. Jeff Sayre loves pasta. April says, "For about seven years we ate pasta every day. So we had lots of pasta shapes in our pantry. In *Noodle Man,* Al Dente is born into a pasta-loving family. His mom and dad run a fresh pasta deli. His grandpa invents pasta shapes and his grandmother knits sweaters from spaghetti."

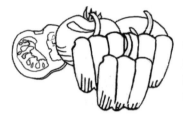

A most popular pasta dish in the United States is Mac & Cheese. Here is a simple recipe to which you can add chopped peppers (red and green make a festive dish), tomatoes, browned hamburger, tuna, or shredded chicken—actually anything you think would make a tasteful addition.

Mac & Cheese

Mix together:

- 1/2 cup (1 stick) butter, melted
- 1 can evaporated milk
- 1 can cheddar cheese soup

Pour this mixture into a baking dish.

Cook 2 1/2 cups elbow macaroni (or any other shaped pasta), and drain.

Mix macaroni with the butter, evaporated milk, and cheddar cheese soup mixture. Add 1/2 pound white American cheese, broken into pieces. Pour into a baking dish.

Top with mixture of butter, bread crumbs, and parmesan cheese and bake at 350° F for 30 minutes.

Pasta Facts

Pasta is thought to have originated in Asia and the Mediterranean, but its popularity has taken it to many parts of the world.

The word pasta is the Italian word for "paste," and while most pasta is made of wheat flour, it is made from flour of other grains as well. All pasta is made of flour mixed with water. Pasta comes in many shapes, and each shape's name reflects the Italian word for that shape. The various shapes are created by passing the dough through molds and tubes that form the shape and size of the pasta.

The shape of the noodles determines the name of the pasta:

- Spaghetti, from spago, "cord"
- Linguini, "little tongues"
- Vermicelli, "little worms"
- Conchiglie, "shells"
- Rigatoni, "furrows," short, wide fluted tubes

- Lasagna, broad, sometime ruffled, ribbons of pasta (from Latin for "pot")
- Fettucine, "small ribbons"
- Ravioli, "little turnips"
- Rotini, "spirals" or "twists"
- Capellini (angel hair), "fine hairs"
- Fusilli, "little spindles" (spirals)
- Penne, "quills"
- Tortellini, "little cakes"
- Cannelloni, tube-or cane-shaped pasta

Soup-er Pasta

A traditional soup in Panama is a soup containing meat, large boiled potatoes, green beans, and a few pieces of 2-inch corn on the cob (those are taken out and nibbled when the soup is eaten). All the ingredients are kept warm in a clear meat broth. This is a pasta-laden variation.

Prepare a simple broth soup (canned broth works, too). Depending on your own preferences, tomato soup, chicken broth, or beef broth are delicious choices. While the broth soup is cooking, chop up a lot of vegetables and other ingredients. Almost any items can be used, but some favorites include:

- Corn on the cob (use 2-inch pieces, or cut the corn off the cob)
- Roasted peppers
- Diced red and green peppers
- Cottage cheese (if using tomato soup)
- Diced mozzarella or cheddar cheese
- Parmesan cheese
- Roasted or fried onions
- Slivered herbs—such as basil and parsley
- Quickly stir-fried or steamed vegetables—zucchini, tomatoes
- Halved cherry tomatoes
- Potatoes

Cook small pasta of several shapes and colors: tubetti, farfalle, and macaroni are favorites.

Put platters or bowls of the ingredients—the pasta, vegetables, and other soup additives—on a buffet table or on the table with serving forks and spoons. Serve each guest with a soup bowl filled with steaming hot soup to which they will select and add from the array of available ingredients.

Signature Recipe—April Pulley Sayre

Selected Books Written by April Pulley Sayre

Crocodile Listens. Illustrated by JoEllen McAllister Stammen. (Greenwillow, 2001)

Dig, Wait, Listen: A Desert Toads Tale. Illustrated by Barbara Bash. (Greenwillow, 2001)

Good Morning, Africa. (Millbrook, 2003)

Noodle Man: The Pasta Superhero. Illustrated by Stephen Costanza. (Orchard Books, 2001)

One Is a Snail, Ten Is a Crab: A Counting by Feet Book. With Jeff Sayre. Illustrated by Randy Cecil. (Candlewick, 2003)

Turtle, Turtle, Watch Out. Illustrated by Lee Christiansen. (Orchard Books, 2000)

Pasta—From Field to Food

Egan, Robert. *Wheat to Pasta* (Changes). (Children's Press, 1997)

Jones, Carol. *Pasta and Noodles* (The Foodmakers). (Chelsea House, 2002)

Julius, Jennifer. *I Like Pasta* (Welcome Books: Good Food). (Children's Press, 2001)

Mayo, Gretchen. *Pasta* (Where Does Our Food Come From?). (Weekly Reader Early Learning Library, 2004)

Janet Stevens—Vegetable Soup

When I agreed to illustrate To Market, To Market, *I decided to set the book in my own messy kitchen and my neighborhood grocery store, the Ideal Market.*

—Janet Stevens

Janet Stevens

Birthday: January 17

Favorite place: Mountains and the ocean

Favorite foods: Chips and salsa, popcorn, oatmeal raisin cookies

Family:

   Spouse—Ted Habermann

   Son—Blake Habermann

   Daughter—Lindsay Habermann

Home:

   Childhood home—Many different places; too numerous to list (military family)

   Now—Boulder, Colorado

Janet Stevens was born in Dallas, Texas, but because her dad was a naval officer, she lived all over the United States. Her childhood was spent in Texas, Massachusetts, Maine, Virginia, Rhode Island, Florida, and finally Hawaii, where she graduated from high school. Because she was seldom in a place long enough to make many friends, she turned to art. She drew from the time she was very young. She loved animals and often drew them in her pictures. (Nowadays, she sometimes sneaks her favorite animal, the wrinkly rhinoceros, into her books—but her editor takes him out.) Many of her animal characters are dressed in clothes from her family's closets. Her characters are seen wearing one of her husband's Hawaiian-print shirts or some of Stevens's jewelry. Hare in *The Tortoise and the Hare* wears her husband's pink tie and her daughter's pink bunny slippers while eating breakfast at the Stevens's table.

A full-time writer and illustrator for many years, Stevens works in her studio, which is just off her kitchen, in the Boulder, Colorado, home where she lives with her family. Together the family enjoys being outdoors. Janet likes to hike, bike, ski, walk her dog (she got her first dog at age forty-four), read, and paint for fun. In the past few years, she has begun to collaborate on books with her sister, Susan Stevens Crummel. Together they have written several books, collaborating electronically between Susan's home in Texas and Janet's home in Colorado.

Janet Stevens (left) and
Susan Crummel Stevens

Vegetable Manifesto Lettuce Salad

In Stevens's book *Tops and Bottoms*, Hare plants all types of vegetables: potatoes, corn, celery, lettuce, and carrots. Use your choice of vegetables to create a scrumptious Greek lettuce salad.

- 1 head lettuce
- Raw vegetables
- 1 to 3 spring onions
- 3 tablespoons olive oil
- 1 tablespoon white vinegar
- 1/2 teaspoon salt
- 1 pinch black pepper
- 1/2 teaspoon basil
- 1/2 teaspoon chopped garlic

Wash lettuce and separate the leaves. Allow lettuce to drain in a colander. To the lettuce add chopped vegetables of your choosing: carrots, celery, tomatoes, radishes, and peppers. Beat the rest of the ingredients in a bowl. Add lettuce leaves and vegetables and turn ingredients gently so that all the leaves and vegetables become coated with the dressing. Serves 4.

Vegetable Potato Soup for Fifteen

Vegetables show up in several books illustrated by Janet Stevens. In *To Market, To Market*, the woman ends up with all kinds of animals in her house and then goes back to the market to buy vegetables to make soup for all her new furred and feathered friends. *Tops and Bottoms* has Hare planting many vegetables. Look for vegetables in her other books, too.

Put 12 cups water and 2 large potatoes, peeled and quartered, in a large soup pot.

Bring water to boil and then add one 14.5-ounce can of whole peeled tomatoes, mashed.

Add:

- 1/4 cup pearl barley
- 1/4 cup uncooked white rice

Cook another 10 minutes until potatoes are soft.

Remove potatoes and mash together with 2 tablespoons margarine, set aside.

Add to the stock pot and cook for 10 minutes until carrots are tender:

- 1/4 teaspoon salt
- 1/4 teaspoon ground black pepper
- 1 large carrot, diced

When carrots are tender, add the following ingredients and cook another 10 minutes:

- 1 onion, chopped
- 1 large stalk celery, with leaves, finely chopped
- 1/2 cup fresh green beans, cut into 1/2 inch pieces
- 3 large potatoes, peeled and diced
- 1/2 cup frozen petite peas, thawed
- 1/2 cup broccoli florets
- 1/4 cup barley flakes

Finally, add back in the mashed potatoes; and then add 1/4 cup barley flakes. Cook for 5 minutes and serve.

Selected Books Written/Illustrated by Janet Stevens

Anansi and the Talking Melon. Text by Eric Kimmel. (Holiday House, 1994)

And the Dish Ran Away with the Spoon. Text by Susan Stevens Crummel and Janet Stevens. (Harcourt, 2001)

Cook-A-Doodle-Doo! Text by Susan Stevens Crummel and Janet Stevens. (Harcourt, 1999)

From Pictures to Words: A Book about Making a Book. (Holiday House, 1995)

Goldilocks and the Three Bears. (Holiday House, 1986)

Jackalope. Text by Susan Stevens Crummel and Janet Stevens. (Harcourt, 2003)

My Big Dog. Text by Susan Stevens Crummel and Janet Stevens. (Golden Books, 2005)

Plaidypus Lost. Text by Susan Stevens Crummel and Janet Stevens. (Holiday House, 2004)

To Market, To Market. Text by Anne Miranda. (Harcourt Brace, 1997)

Tops and Bottoms. (Harcourt Brace, 1995)

Tortoise and the Hare. Retold from Aesop. (Holiday House, 1984)

Tumbleweed Stew. Text by Susan Stevens Crummel and Janet Stevens. (Harcourt, 2000)

Why Epossumondas Has No Hair on His Tail. Text by Coleen Salley. (Harcourt Brace, 2004)

Books about Vegetables and Nutrition

Ehlert, Lois. *Growing Vegetable Soup.* (Harcourt, 1987)

Ehlert, Lois. *Eating the Alphabet: Fruits & Vegetables from A to Z.* (Harcourt, 1989)

Elcare, Melanie. *A Harvest of Color: Growing a Vegetable Garden.* (Ragged Bear USA, 2002)

Leedy, Loreen. *The Edible Pyramid: Good Eating Every Day.* (Holiday House, 1996)

Lin, Grace. *The Ugly Vegetables.* (Charlesbridge, 2001)

Pallotta, Jerry. *The Victory Garden Vegetable Alphabet Book* (Jerry Pallotta's Alphabet Books). (Charlesbridge, 1992)

Robinson, Fay. *Vegetables, Vegetables!* (Rookie Read-About Science). (Children's Press, 1995)

Tanya Lee Stone—Latkes

Photo: Kathy Pintair

Tanya Lee Stone

Birthday: December 23

Favorite place: any beach

**Favorite foods: steamer clams,
chocolate pecan pie, potato latkes**

Family:

   Spouse—Alan Segal

   Son—Jake

   Daughter—Liza

Home:

   Childhood—Milford, Connecticut

   Now—Vermont

*L is for latkes
Crisp, chewy, and hot
Grate up some potatoes,
We'll sure eat a lot!*

**—from *D Is for Dreidel: A Hanukkah
Alphabet Book* by Tanya Lee Stone**

Tanya Lee Stone often makes latkes for her family—the recipe she uses is her grandmother's. (The photo beside Stone in this picture is that of her grandmother.)

"When asked to recall a favorite food story from my life, I was hard-pressed to settle on just one. Food has always been one of the major backdrops of my family's life stage. How can I possibly choose between the drama of the full-blown Medieval holiday dinner my father and uncle staged, with gold-leafed, calligraphy menus and sides of beef hanging from the kitchen ceiling? Or the comfort-laden bowls full of mushroom, barley, and kielbasa soup ladled out for me each time I returned home from college? Or the bushels of corn we kids would shuck on the front porch on summer evenings? Or our neighborhood beachfront clam bakes with foil-wrapped potatoes, salt-of-the-earth quahog clams, and delicate steamers? The memories of these sights, tastes, and smells flooded my senses as my mind reeled with the task of choosing just one food story for this book.

"But the one that won fills my heart with more than tastes and smells, and feeds my soul with memories of my cherished and deeply missed grandmother Sarah (aka Sally, Sadie—or to all her grandkids—Grammy). Grammy showed her love every day, in all kinds of ways. But making latkes was one of the most delicious! Crispy on the outside, chewy on the inside, every mouth-watering bite of her latkes was infused with love. You didn't even mind the tiny bit you always burned your tongue and roof of your mouth, as patiently waiting to sink your teeth into that first fresh-from-the-frying pan latke before it cooled just wasn't an option for any of us."

—Tanya Lee Stone

Barley and Mushroom Kielbasa Soup

Tanya Lee Stone remembers fondly a variation of this soup served at her family table on days she returned home from college. Kielbasa is a spicy Polish sausage.

Put 1 tablespoon olive oil in a large pot and sauté for 3 to 4 minutes.

- 1/4 pound small button mushrooms, cut in half
- 1 medium onion, chopped
- 3 cloves of garlic, finely chopped

Stir occasionally and add:

- 2 teaspoons dried leaf oregano, crushed
- 2 teaspoons dried leaf basil, crushed

Sauté 2 additional minutes and then stir in:

- 6 cups fat-free chicken broth
- 1 cup pearl barley
- 2 bay leaves

Bring to boil, then reduce heat, and simmer for 25 minutes. Mix in:

- Another 1/4 pound of button mushrooms, cut in half
- 3 medium carrots, peeled and sliced 1/4 inch thick
- 1/2 cup chicken broth

Bring to a boil a second time. Reduce heat and simmer for another 20 minutes.

Add 1 pound fat-reduced Kielbasa sausage, cut into 1/2-inch-thick slices.

Cook on medium heat for another 5 minutes.

Remove bay leaves; and serve. Makes about 8 servings.

Chocolate Pecan Pie

Add 2 large eggs to:

- 1 1/2 cups sugar
- less than a pinch of salt
- 3 1/2 tablespoons cocoa

Mix well and then stir in:

- 1/2 tablespoon vanilla
- 1/2 can evaporated milk (6-ounce can)
- 1/2 stick (2 ounces) melted butter (may substitute margarine)

Pour into pie shell, sprinkle 1/2 cup pecan halves on top.

Bake at 350° F for 40 to 45 minutes.

Tanya's Grandmother's Latkes

- 12 large potatoes
- 2 onions
- 4 eggs
- 1 teaspoon baking powder
- 2 teaspoons salt
- 1 teaspoon pepper
- 2/3 cup flour

Grate potatoes on the coarse side of a grater. Squeeze the juice out of the grated potatoes to make them nice and dry. Grate the onion. Add eggs, salt, pepper, and baking powder. Use some or all of the flour for soaking up extra liquid.

Heat about 1/4 inch of oil in a pan, fry on moderate heat until crisp on one side, flip and repeat. You need to keep a fair amount of oil in the pan, don't try to fry them too fast, it takes a lot longer than pancakes. Drain on paper towels. Serve with sour cream/applesauce.

Signature Recipe—Tanya Lee Stone

Selected Books written by Tanya Lee Stone

Crocodilians (Wild Wild World). (Blackbirch Press, 2004)

D Is for Dreidel: A Hanukkah Alphabet Book. (Price Stern Sloan, 2003)

Ilan Ramon: Israel's First Astronaut. (Kar-Ben, 2003; reprint)

Kangaroos (Wild Wild World). (Blackbirch Press, 2003)

Lions (Wild Wild World). (Blackbirch Press, 2004)

Living in a World of Blue: Where Survival Means Blending In (Living in a World Of . . .). (Blackbirch Press, 2001)

M Is for Mistletoe: A Christmas Alphabet Book. (Price Stern Sloan, 2003)

P Is for Passover: A Holiday Alphabet Book. (Price Stern Sloan, 2003)

Soups * Soups * Soups

During Tanya's college years soup (especially the Barley and Mushroom Kielbasa Soup featured here) was comfort food. In the United States, January is designated as National Soup Month. Here are some soup books that might be good reading on the day you fix soup or anytime during January.

Brown, Marcia. *Stone Soup.* (Atheneum, 1947; many editions)

Cooper, Helen. *Pumpkin Soup.* (Farrar, Straus & Giroux, 1999)

Creech, Sharon. *Granny Torrelli Makes Soup.* (Joanna Cotler, 2003)

DiCamillo, Kate. *Tale of Despereaux: Being the Story of a Mouse, a Princess, Some Soup, and a Spool of Thread* (Newbery Medal Book). (Candlewick, 2003; soup plays a part in this novel, but the book is not about soup)

Ehlert, Lois. *Growing Vegetable Soup.* (Harcourt Brace Jovanovich, 1987)

Forest, Heather. *Stone Soup.* Illustrated by Susan Gaber. (August House LittleFolk, 2000)

McGovern, Ann. *Stone Soup.* Illustrated by Winslow Pinney Pels. (Scholastic, 1986)

Rylant, Cynthia. *Mr. Putter & Tabby Stir the Soup.* Illustrated by Arthur Howard. (Harcourt, 2003)

Sendak, Maurice. *Chicken Soup with Rice: A Book of Months.* (HarperCollins, 1962)

Anastasia Suen—Chocolate Chip Cookies

My favorite lunch when I was growing up was ham on rye, a yellow pear and three chocolate chip cookies. The ham was salty, the pear was juicy, and the cookies were sweet. It was the perfect combination!

—**Anastasia Suen**

Anastasia Suen

Birthday: January 22

Favorite place: The beach

Favorite foods: Pineapples, strawberries, any type of chocolate and cheesecake.

Family:

Spouse—Clifford

Son—Nathan

Daughter—Aimée

Home:

Childhood—Florida and California

Now—Texas

Anastasia Suen grew up in a household with six other children, three brothers and three sisters. On school days her mom woke up early and made their lunches before the children woke up. At lunchtime, Anastasia would find out what was in her lunch. She says, "I had homemade cookies in my lunch, everyday. There were always three of them. It was our dessert. The only question was: which ones would they be?"

Anastasia's mother often made pineapple upside down cake after church on Sundays. She experimented with cheesecake recipes for weeks until she found one that she liked. Anastasia and her brothers and sisters happily ate all of her test cheesecakes.

When Anastasia went off to college, she took her mother's chocolate chip cookie recipe and studied to become a teacher. After graduating, she began teaching first grade and wrote "little readers" for her students. Later she taught fifth graders and wrote plays for them to perform. Eventually, when her own children were born, she stopped teaching but kept on writing. Just like her favorite cookies that had come in threes, so did her first acceptance letters. When her daughter was in kindergarten, three acceptance letters came on one day—three magazines wanted to publish articles she had written. Two years later she sold three book manuscripts in a three-month period. Now she has written more than thirty books for young readers, many of them information books. She and her family live in Texas where she finds ideas all around her. She says, "You don't have to leave home to write. Just write what you see."

PINEAPPLE UPSIDE-DOWN CAKE TRIVIA

Pineapple wasn't used widely for upside-down cake until 1925. In fact, the term "upside-down cake" wasn't often used until after the middle of the nineteenth century, but the style of baking is thought to date back much further, probably to the Middle Ages. The earliest of fruit upside-down cakes were made in cast-iron skillets on top of the stove. Jim Dole invented the concept of canning pineapple in 1903, and sometime after that the classic cake was created. In 1925, the Hawaiian Pineapple Company (now Dole Pineapple) held a contest for pineapple recipes. The winning recipes were to be printed in a cookbook. Sixty thousand recipes were entered—2,500 of them were for Pineapple Upside-Down cake. Today the Hawaiian Islands are the leading producers of pineapples.

Pineapple Upside-Down Cake

The earliest upside-down cakes were skillet cakes, but we cook ours in a 9 x 12–inch cake pan (to accommodate a commercial cake mix). The cakes entered in the 1925 Hawaiian Pineapple Company contest were made from scratch. Cake mixes are much improved these days, so we use a mix instead of scratch baking, but if you have a favorite cake recipe, use that instead.

Pineapple Topping

Drain 12 canned pineapple rings and put on a paper towel to dry completely.

Lightly butter a 9 x 12–inch square cake pan and sprinkle 1 cup of packed light or dark brown sugar in the bottom of the pan.

Randomly place one stick of butter, sliced and chunked on the brown sugar.

Place the pineapple rings (or thoroughly drained crushed pineapple) in three rows of four on top of the brown sugar.

In the middle of each pineapple ring, place a maraschino cherry. Lightly spoon the prepared cake batter onto the pineapple and bake according to the instructions of the mix or cake recipe. The cake is done when it springs back to the touch, and a toothpick (except for the tip) comes out dry when inserted into the cake.

MY MOTHER'S CHOCOLATE CHIP COOKIES

Anastasia Suen's mother is French, and so, Suen says, "We always ended our meal with something sweet. We had homemade cookies, pie, or cake everyday. When I went off to college, I carefully copied her recipe for chocolate chip cookies. The recipe is doubled, so it makes five dozen cookies. With seven kids, that didn't last very long!"

Anastasia's Mother's Chocolate Chip Cookies

Cream until fluffy:

- 1 cup shortening
- 1/2 cup granulated sugar
- 1 cup brown sugar
- 1 teaspoon vanilla
- Add 2 eggs well beaten

Sift:

- 2 cups and 4 level tablespoons sifted flour
- 1 teaspoon soda

Combine flour mixture with creamed ingredients. Add 1 cup chocolate chips.

Use a spoon to drop cookie dough onto a greased baking sheet. Bake in a preheated oven at 375° F for 10 minutes. Recipe makes 5 dozen.

Signature Recipe—Anastasia Suen

Selected Books written by Anastasia Suen

Baby Born. Illustrated by Chih-wei Chang. (Lee & Low, 1999)

Hamster Chase (2001); *Willie's Birthday* (2001); *The Clubhouse* (2002); *Loose Tooth* (2002) (A series of books based on characters created by Ezra Jack Keats); Illustrated by Allan Eitzen. (Viking)

Picture Writing: A New Approach to Writing for Kids & Teens (Writer's Digest Books, 2003)

Raise the Roof. Illustrated by Elwood H. Smith. (Viking, 2003)

Red Light, Green Light. Illustrated by Ken Wilson-Max. (Harcourt, 2005)

Subway. Illustrated by Karen Katz. (Viking, 2004)

Toddler Two. Illustrated by Winnie Chean. (Lee & Low, 2000)

Cake Connections

Just as pineapple upside-down cake held a traditional place in Anastasia Suen's childhood, these books hold special memories or are part of significant events in the character's life. Read these books and discover the "cake" connection.

Beil, Karen Magnuson. *A Cake All for Me!* (Holiday House, 1998)

Carick, Carol. *Upside-down Cake.* (Houghton Mifflin, 1999)

Cohen, Barbara. *Make a Wish Molly.* (Yearling, 1995)

Joseph, Lynn. *Jasmine's Parlour Day.* Illustrated by Ann Grifalconi. (HarperCollins, 1994)

London, Jonathan. *Froggy Bakes a Cake.* (Scholastic, 2000)

Parish, Peggy. *Amelia Bedelia Helps Out.* Illustrated by Lynn Sweat. (Greenwillow, 1979)

Parish, Peggy. *Good Work, Amelia Bedelia.* Illustrated by Lynn Sweat. (Greenwillow, 1976)

Parish, Peggy. *Merry Christmas, Amelia Bedelia.* Illustrated by Lynn Sweat. (Greenwillow, 1986)

Polacco, Patricia. *Thunder Cake.* (Scholastic, 1990)

Jane Yolen and Heidi Elizabet Yolen Stemple—Chocolate

Photo: David Stemple

Now that we work as writers together on books like our Unsolved Mysteries from History series or our poetry book called Dear Mother, Dear Daughter, we get to sit and talk about books with our favorite drink.

—Heidi Elizabet Yolen Stemple

Jane Yolen

Birthday: February 11

Favorite place: Scotland

Favorite foods: Chocolate Cake

Family:

Spouse—David Stemple

Daughter—Heidi Elisabet Yolen Stemple

Sons—Adam Douglas Stemple, Jason Frederic Stemple

Home:

Childhood—New York City and Westport, Connecticut

Now—Hatfield, Massachusetts and Scotland

Heidi Elisabet Yolen Stemple

Birthday: July 1

Favorite place: Scotland and the Galapagos Islands

Favorite foods: Gyros, grape leaves, olives, all things chocolate, key lime pie, and Twinkies

Family:

Daughters—Maddison Jane and Glendon Alexandria

Home:

Childhood—Massachusetts

Now—Massachusetts (but lived in the south for eighteen years: Florida, South Carolina, Texas, and Georgia)

Jane Yolen has been called the Hans Christian Andersen of America. Certainly, she is an accomplished and versatile author, and her talent is undisputable—she has written fiction and information books, picture books and novels for older readers, prose and poetry.

Jane and her brother grew up in a household where their parents, Will Hyatt Yolen and Isabel Yolen, both writers, encouraged their children's interests. Jane Yolen wrote entire plays and musicals at a young age. After her college years, she moved to Greenwich Village in New York, with two roommates, and worked in publishing before becoming a freelance writer. It was at a party at her apartment where she met a friend of one of her roommates, David Stemple. They married, and after taking a year off to travel, the couple settled in western Massachusetts where Stemple took a job at the University of Massachusetts Computer Center in Amherst. They raised their three children on an old tobacco farm in Hatfield, Massachusetts. Jane and David, who is retired now from the University of Massachusetts, spend part of the year in Massachusetts and part in Scotland. Jane continues to tell and write stories wherever she is.

Royal Chocolate Cake

- 8 ounces dark semisweet chocolate
- 2/3 cup butter
- 1 cup sugar
- 4 eggs
- 4 heaped tablespoons flour
- 4 tablespoons unsweetened cocoa powder
- 2 teaspoons baking powder
- 1 teaspoon vanilla extract
- 1/4 cup sour cream

Melt the chocolate with the butter in a double boiler; over hot water. While the chocolate is melting, beat the eggs with sugar, mix with flour, cocoa powder, baking powder, and vanilla extract. Slowly fold in the melted butter and chocolate mixture and the sour cream. Pour the batter in a 9-inch round cake pan (lined with baking paper or grease the bottom).

Bake in a 350° F oven for 50 minutes or until a wooden pick inserted in center comes out clean.

Cool the cake. Remove the crusted surface on the top of the cake, and cut in half, horizontally.

Chocolate-Chocolate Frosting

Heat 2/3 cup heavy cream or whipping cream in a saucepan.

Remove from heat, add 9 ounces (260 g) of finely chopped dark semisweet chocolate, and stir until smooth.

Place part of the frosting in the middle of the cake layers, place top portion of the layer on top of the frosted layer, and drizzle remainder on the top of the cake in such a way that the frosting drips over the sides.

Jane Yolen's husband, David Stemple, often took their three children owling near their rural Massachusetts home. Those wonder filled evenings were the inspiration for the story Yolen wrote in the early 1980s. The story *Owl Moon* was illustrated by John Schoenherr, who was awarded the prestigious Caldecott Medal (1988) for the watercolors he created for the book. The Pa in the illustrations was Jane's husband (and Heidi's dad); the little girl was based on Heidi. When Jane wrote the story, she imagined the setting to be her acreage beside the Stemple home. Schoenherr however, based the wooded area on his own New Jersey farm.

"*Owl Moon* is a made up story about our real lives. Our whole family has been out owling with the real life Pa. We are crazy for chocolate, and there is nothing better to warm you up after patiently looking and listening for owls on a cold New England night than hot chocolate."

—Heidi Elizabet Yolen Stemple

Hot Chocolate

In a pot, combine 6 ounces of sweet cooking chocolate, 6 cups of milk, 2 teaspoons cinnamon, and 2 teaspoons sugar. Cook the mixture in a pot over medium-high heat. Stir it constantly until the chocolate melts and the mixture is blended. Let it sit boiling until the top begins to foam and rise. Then, remove from the stovetop, and stir it again. Serves six. (Recipe compliments of Katherine Hanson.)

Selected Books by Jane Yolen/Heidi Elisabet Yolen Stemple

Dear Mother, Dear Daughter: Poems for Young People by Jane Yolen and Heidi E. Y. Stemple. Illustrated by Gil Ashby. (Wordsong/Boyds Mills Press, 2001)

Firebird by Jane Yolen. Illustrated by Vladimir Vagin. (HarperCollins, 2002)

Horizons: Poems As Far As the Eye Can See by Jane Yolen. Photographs by Jason Stemple. (Wordsong/Boyds Mills, 2002)

Least Things: Poems about Small Natures by Jane Yolen. Photographs by Jason Stemple. (Wordsong/Boyds Mills, 2003)

Meow: Cat Stories from around the World by Jane Yolen. Illustrated by Hala Wittwer. (HarperCollins, 2004)

Mirror, Mirror by Jane Yolen and Heidi E.Y. Stemple. (Viking, 2000)

Owl Moon by Jane Yolen Illustrated by John Schoenherr. (Philomel, 1987)

Roanoke: The Lost Colony: An Unsolved Mystery from History by Jane Yolen and Heidi E.Y. Stemple. Illustrated by Roger Roth. (Simon & Schuster, 2003)

The Wolf Girls: An Unsolved Mystery from History by Jane Yolen and Heidi E.Y. Stemple. Illustrated by Roger Roth. (Simon & Schuster, 2000)

Chocolate Books

Among Jane Yolen's favorite foods is a chocolate cake, and Heidi E. Y. Stemple likes "all things chocolate"—not unlike authors such as Robert Kimmel and James Howe, self-proclaimed chocoholics. These books might be reading material for other chocoholics.

Adler, David A. *Cam Jansen and the Chocolate Fudge Mystery* (Cam Jansen Adventure). Illustrated by Susanna Natti. (Viking, 1993)

Blumenthal, Deborah. *The Chocolate-Covered-Cookie Tantrum.* (Clarion, 1999)

Catling, Patrick Skene. *The Chocolate Touch.* (HarperCollins, 1979)

Gwynne, Fred. *A Chocolate Moose for Dinner.* (Prentice-Hall, 1987)

Henkes, Kevin. *Lilly's Chocolate Heart.* (HarperFestival, 2003)

Kimmel, Robert. *Chocolate Fever.* (Putnam, 1989; reprint)

Warner, Gertrude Chandler. *The Chocolate Sundae Mystery* (Boxcar Children Mysteries). Illustrated by Charles Tang. (Albert Whitman, 1993)

Photograph Credits

Photograph of David A. Adler by Nina Crews, courtesy of David A. Adler.

Photograph of Laurie Halse Anderson by Sharron L. McElmeel.

Photograph of Caroline Arnold by Sharron L. McElmeel.

Photograph of Caroline Arnold in the Mesa Verde by Richard Hewett. Courtesy of Caroline Arnold.

Photograph of Jim Aylesworth by Sharron L. McElmeel.

Photograph of Mary Azarian by John Guare. Courtesy of Mary Azarian.

Photograph of Bob Barner by Sharron L. McElmeel.

Photograph of Raymond Bial, courtesy of Raymond Bial.

Photograph of Ashley Bryan by Sharron L. McElmeel.

Photograph of Eve Bunting, courtesy of Eve Bunting.

Photograph of Dori Hillstead Butler, courtesy of Dori Hillstead Butler.

Photograph of Toni Buzzeo by Sharron L. McElmeel.

Photograph of Janie Bynum, courtesy of Janie Bynum.

Photograph of Eric Carle by Sharron L. McElmeel.

Photograph of Mary Casanova by Charles Casanova. Courtesy of Mary Casanova.

Photograph of Judith Caseley by Michael Curtis. Courtesy of Judith Caseley.

Photograph of Shirley Climo by Al Weisberger. Courtesy of Shirley Climo.

Photograph of Susan Stevens Crummel. Courtesy of Susan Stevens Crummel.

Photograph of Susan Stevens Crummel and Janet Stevens, courtesy of Susan Stevens Crummel.

Photograph of Janet Stevens, courtesy of Janet Stevens.

Photograph of Pat Cummings by Ai Miki 2002. Courtesy of Pat Cummings.

Photograph of Carl Deuker by Anne Mitchell. Courtesy of Carl Deuker.

Photograph of Diane Dillon, courtesy of Diane Dillon.

Photograph of Leo Dillon, courtesy of Leo Dillon.

Photograph of Marianne J. Dyson, courtesy of Marianne J. Dyson.

Photograph of Kathy Feeney by R. J. Kwap. Courtesy of Kathy Feeney.

Photograph of Debra Frasier by Sharron L. McElmeel.

Photograph of Gail Gibbons by Kent Ancliffe. Courtesy of Gail Gibbons.

Photograph of Paul Goble by Janet Goble. Courtesy of Paul Goble.

Photograph of Carol Gorman by Sharron L. McElmeel.

Photograph of Dan Gutman, courtesy of Dan Gutman.

Photograph of Esther Hershenhorn by Kevin Hammett. Courtesy of Esther Hershenhorn.

Photograph of Trina Schart Hyman and Katrin Tchana by John Layton. Courtesy of Katrin Tchana and Trina Schart Hyman.

Photograph of Paul Brett Johnson, courtesy of Paul Brett Johnson.

Photograph of Keiko Kasza, courtesy of Keiko Kasza.

Photograph of Steven Kellogg by Sharron L. McElmeel.

Photograph of Jane Kurtz, courtesy of Jane Kurtz.

Photograph of Elaine Landau by Devon Cass. Courtesy of Elaine Landau.

Photograph of Deborah Nourse Lattimore by Nicholas Lattimore. Courtesy of Deborah Nourse Lattimore.

Photograph of Melinda Long, courtesy of Melinda Long.

Photograph of Betsy Maestro, courtesy of Betsy Maestro.

Photograph of Jacqueline Briggs Martin, courtesy of Jacqueline Briggs Martin.

Photograph of Yuyi Morales by Tim O'Meara. Courtesy of Yuyi Morales.

Photograph of Nancy Winslow Parker by Dennis O'Grady. Courtesy of Nancy Winslow Parker.

Photograph of the Paterson family, courtesy of John and Katherine Paterson.

Photograph of Jeni Reeves by Sharron L. McElmeel.

Photograph of Dian Curtis Regan by John Regan. Courtesy of Dian Curtis Regan.

Photographs of Barbara Santucci by Jeff Swanberg (p. 177) and Michael Santucci (p. 180). Courtesy of Barbara Santucci.

Photograph of April Pulley Sayre by Jeff Sayre. Courtesy of April Pulley Sayre.

Photograph of Janet Stevens by Sharron L. McElmeel.

Photograph of Tanya Lee Stone by Kathy Pintair. Courtesy of Tanya Lee Stone.

Photograph of Anastasia Suen by Cecil Stringfellow. Courtesy of Anastasia Suen.

Photograph of Jane Yolen and Heidi Elizabet Yolen Stemple by David Stemple. Courtesy of Jane Yolen and Heidi Elizabet Yolen Stemple.

Illustrative Credits

All line drawings in this book were created by Deborah L. McElmeel except as noted below.

Azarian, Mary
Drawing based on illustration from *Miss Bridie Chose a Shovel* by Leslie Connor. Illustrated by Mary Azarian. (Houghton Mifflin, 2004). Used with permission of Mary Azarian.

Bynum, Janie
Drawing of Altoona Baboona in the kitchen from *Altoona Baboona,* written and illustrated by Janie Bynum. (Harcourt, 1999). This black and white drawing used with permission of Janie Bynum.

Goble, Paul
Illustration of Iktomi beating the Buffalo Berries from the bushes with a stick is from *Iktomi and the Buffalo Berries* by Paul Goble (Orchard, 1989). Used with permission.

Hyman, Trina Schart
Illustration of Dragon and the "Honey Rice Cakes to Die for!" created by Trina Schart Hyman. Used with permission.

Kellogg, Steven
   Illustration of Jenny wheeling in the "National Rodent Day" cheesecake was created by Steven Kellogg. Used with permission.

Parker, Nancy Winslow
   The illustration of onions and the sailor, by Nancy Winslow Parker. Used with permission.

Reeves, Jeni
   The illustrations of the skillet, chess pie, and table were created by Jeni Reeves. Used with permission.

Quotation Credits

Adler, David A. Letter to the author, 2004.

Anderson, Laurie Halse. Letter to the author, 2004.

Arnold, Caroline. *The Ancient Cliff Dwellers of Mesa Verde*. Clarion Books, 1992; p. 25.

Arnold, Caroline. Letter to the author, 2004.

Aylesworth, Jim. Letter to the author, 2004.

Azarian, Mary. Letter to the author, 2004.

Barner, Bob. Letter to the author, 2004.

Bial, Raymond. Letter to author, 2004.

Bryan, Ashley. *Turtle Knows Your Name*. Atheneum, 1989.

Bryan, Ashley. Letter to the author, 2004.

Bryan, Ashley. Letter to the author from Elaine Martindale, 2004.

Bunting, Eve. *A Picnic in October*. Harcourt, 1999; p. 5.

Butler, Dori Hillestad. Letter to the author, 2004.

Buzzeo, Toni. *Sea Chest*. Dial Books for Young Readers, 2002; unp.

Bynum, Janie. *Altoona Baboona*. Harcourt, 1999; unp.

Bynum, Janie. Letter to the author, 2004.

Carle, Eric. Undated brochure/newsletter distributed in the early 1990s by Picture Book Studios, circa 1993.

Casanova, Mary. Letter to the author, 2004.

Caseley, Judith. *Sisters*. Greenwillow, 2004.

Caseley, Judith. Letter to the author, 2004.

Climo, Shirley. *The Persian Cinderella*. Clarion, 1996.

Climo, Shirley. Letter to the author, 2004.

Climo, Shirley. *Magic and Mischief: Tales from Cornwall*. Clarion, 1999.

Cummings, Pat. Letter to the author, 2004.

Deuker, Carl. Letter to the author, 2004.

Dillon, Diane and Leo Dillon. *The Girl Who Spun Gold* by Virginia Hamilton. Blue Sky Press, 2000; p. 22–23

Dillon, Diane and Leo Dillon. Letter to the author, 2004.

Dyson, Marianne J. Letter to the author, 2004.

Feeney, Kathy. *Marco Polo: Explorer of China.* Enslow, 2004.

Feeney, Kathy. Letter to the author, 2004.

Frasier, Debra. Letter to the author, 2004.

Gaber, Suan. *Ten Sleepy Sheep* by Phyllis Root. Candlewick, 2004.

Gaber, Susan. Letter to the author, 2004.

Gibbons, Gail. *The Seasons of Arnold's Apple Tree*s. Harcourt, 1984.

Gibbons, Gail. Letter to the author, 2004.

Goble, Paul. Letter to the author, 2004.

Gorman, Carol. *Stumptown Kid* by Carol Gorman and Ron Findley. Peachtree Press, 2005.

Gorman, Carol. Letter to the author, 2004.

Gutman, Dan. Letter to the author, 2004.

Hershenhorn, Esther. Letter to the author, 2004.

Hyman, Trina Schart and Katrin Tchana. Letter to the author from Katrin Tchana, 2004.

Johnson, Paul Brett. Letter to the author, 2004.

Kasza, Keiko. Letter to the author, 2004.

Kellogg, Steven. *Island of the Skog.* Dial, 1973; unp.

Kellogg, Steven. Letter to the author, 2004.

Kurtz, Jane. Letter to the author, 2004.

Landau, Elaine. Letter to the author, 2004.

Lattimore, Deborah Nourse. Letter to the author, 2004.

Long, Melinda. Letter to the author, 2004.

Martin, Jacqueline Briggs. *Sand Island.* Houghton Mifflin, 2003; unp.

Martin, Jacqueline Briggs. Letter to the author, 2004.

Morales, Yuyi. *Just a Minute: a Trickster Tale and Counting Book.* Chronicle, 2003; unp.

Morales, Yuyi. Letter to the author, 2004.

Parker, Nancy Winslow. Letter to the author, 2004.

Paterson, John, and Katherine Paterson. *Blueberries for the Queen.* HarperCollins, 2004; p. 17

Paterson, John, and Katherine Paterson. Letter to the author from Katherine Paterson, 2004.

Reeves, Jeni. Letter to the author, 2004.

Regan, Dian Curtis. Letter to the author, 2004.

Santucci, Barbara. *Abbey's Chairs.* Eerdman, 2004; unp.

Santucci, Barbara. Letter to the author, 2004.

Sayre, April Pulley. Letter to the author, 2004.

Stevens, Janet. Letter to the author, 2004.

Stone, Tanya. *D Is for Dreidel: A Hanukkah Alphabet Book.* Price Stern Sloan, 2003.

Stone, Tanya. Letter to the author, 2004.

Suen, Anastasia. Letter to the author, 2004.

Yolen, Jane, and Heidi Elizabet Yolen Stemple. Letter to the author from Heidi E. Y. Stemple, 2004.

Acknowledgments of Recipe Sources

Except as noted, all recipes in this book were developed and tested by Deborah L. McElmeel, a culinary expert with two decades of experience in the culinary field. McElmeel holds a graduate degree in science and used her knowledge of chemistry and her extensive experience in the restaurant industry to develop and adapt the many recipes in this book.

Arnold, Caroline—Anasazi Bean Soup. Recipe from Caroline Arnold; adapted and reprinted with her permission.

Aylesworth, Jim—Norm's Fudge and Norm's Fudge Balls. Family recipes from Jim Aylesworth; reprinted with his permission.

Barner, Bob—Southern Pecan Pie. Family recipe from Bob Barner. Reprinted with permission.

Bial, Raymond—Raymond's Dill Pickles and German Potato Salad. Family recipes from Raymond Bial. Reprinted with permission.

Bryan, Ashley—Bread Pudding and Sweet Potato Pie. Family recipes from Elaine Martindale, Ashley Bryan's sister and according to her brother, a wonderful cook. Reprinted with permission.

Butler, Dori Hillstead—Dori's Grandmother's Lefse Hardangerlefse and Tom's Potato Lefse Potekaker. Family recipes from Dori Hillstead Butler. Reprinted with permission.

Buzzeo, Toni—Pumpkin Pie Pizzazz. Compliments of McBookwords LLC. Reprinted with permission.

Bynum, Janie—Banana Bread. Compliments of Janie Bynum. Reprinted with permission.

Carle, Eric—German Style Potato Dumplings. Compliments of Elsie Oehler. Recipe originally published in *The Ronneburg Recipe Album: German Style Cooking* Amana, Iowa, Ronneburg Restaurant, Inc., 1981. Permission obtained with the kind assistance of Yana Cutler, co-owner and proprietor of *The Ronneburg Restaurant and Shops* in Amana (http://www.theronneburg.com). Reprinted with permission.

Casanova, Mary—Crazy Chocolate Cake. Compliments of Mary Casanova from her friends Dorothy and Ione. Reprinted with permission.

Caseley, Judith—Rocco's Broccoli So That You Can Eat Ice Cream Later. Compliments of Judith Caseley and her friend Rocco from the Italian men's club. Reprinted with permission.

Crummel, Susan Stevens—Mexican Roll-ups. Compliments of Susan Stevens Crummel.

Dyson, Marianne J.—Saffron Chicken. Compliments of Marianne J. Dyson.

Hurwitz, Johanna—Blueberry Soup. Compliments of Johanna Hurwitz from the guide on the Llama trek through Vermont.

Kasza, Keiko—Potato Salad. A family recipe compliments of Keiko Kasza.

Kurtz, Jane—Orange Spirals. A family recipe compliments of Jane Kurtz.

Lattimore, Deborah Nourse—Shrimp Santorini. Compliments of Deborah Nourse Lattimore.

Martin, Jacqueline Briggs—Coconut Cream Cake. Compliments of Jacqueline Briggs Martin.

Paterson, John, and Katherine Paterson—Blueberry Muffins. Compliments of Katherine Paterson.

Reeves, Jeni—Chess Pie and Skillet Cornbread. Family recipes compliments of Jeni Reeves.

Regan, Dian Curtis—Curtis Brownies. Family recipe compliments of Dian Curtis Regan.

Santucci, Barbara—Zucchini Bread. Compliments of Barbara Santucci.

Sayre, April Pulley—Soup-er Pasta. Compliments of April Pulley Sayre.

Stone, Tanya—Tanya's Grandmothers Latkes. Family recipe compliments of Tanya Stone.

Suen, Anastasia. Anastasia's Mother's Chocolate Chip Cookies. Family recipe compliments of Anastasia Suen.

Yolen, Jane, and Heide E. Y. Stemple. Hot Chocolate. Recipe compliments of Katherine Hanson.

Sources for More Information

Many of the authors and illustrators featured in this book, *Authors in the Kitchen: Recipes, Stories, and More,* also host their own Web sites, which provide additional information about them and their books. Hot links to those sites that are available may be found on the Author Links page at http://www.mcelmeel.com/curriculum/authorlinks.html.

In addition, a companion page for this book is available at http://www.mcelmeel.com/writing/authorsinthekitchen.html. On this site, you will find hot links to a variety of Web pages that may provide you with additional information to topics connected to various books/recipes in this book.

General Index

100 Days Tales (booklist), 128

Abby's Chairs, 177
acknowledgments of recipe sources, 205–6
Adler, David, 1–4, 4 (booklist)
Altoona Baboona, 45
Amana, Iowa, 51
Ambrosia, 89, 91
Anasazi (booklist), 10
Anasazi beans, 10
Anasazi, 10
Ancient Cliff Dwellers of Mesa Verde, The, 9
And the Dish Ran Away with the Spoon, 65
Anderson, Laurie Halse, 5–8, 6 (booklist)
Angel Food Cake, 14
Antiqua, 30
Apostle Islands, 153
Apple Books (booklist), 100
Arnold, Caroline, 9–12, 12 (booklist)
Aylesworth, Jim, 13–16, 16 (booklist)
Azarian, Mary, xi, 17–20, 20 (booklist)

Baking Cinnamon Rolls, 18
Baking Mishaps (booklist), 4
Baking Mishaps, 4
bananas, 46
Barner, Bob, 21–24, 24 (booklist)
Bartholdi, Frederic-Auguste, 35
Baseball Cards—More Stories and
    Information (booklist), 111
Baseball Facts—Fact or Fable?, 110
Berry Book, The, 98
Bial, Raymond, 25–28, 28 (booklist)
birthday cakes, 1, 2
birthday celebration, 2
Blueberry Muffins, 165
Booklists (authors and illustrators)
    David A. Adler, 4
    Laurie Halse Anderson, 6
    Caroline Arnold, 12
    Jim Aylesworth, 16

Mary Azarian, 20
Bob Barner, 24
Raymond Bial, 28
Ashley Bryan, 32
Eve Bunting, 36
Dori Hillestad Butler, 40
Toni Buzzeo, 44
Janie Bynum, 48
Eric Carle, 50
Mary Casanova, 56
Judith Caseley, 60
Shirley Climo, 63
Susan Stevens Crummel, 68
Pat Cummings, 71–72
Carl Deuker, 76
Leo Dillon and Diane Dillon, 79
Marianne Dyson, 84
Kathy Feeney, 88
Debra Frasier, 92
Susan Gaber, 96
Gail Gibbons, 99–100
Paul Goble, 104
Carol Gorman, 108
Dan Gutman, 112
Esther Herschenhorn, 116
Trina Schart Hyman/Katrin Tchana,
    120
Paul Brett Johnson, 123
Keiko Kasza, 127
Steven Kellogg, 132
Jane Kurtz, 136
Elaine Landau, 140
Deborah Lattimore, 144
Melinda Long, 145
Betsy Maestro, 149
Jacqueline Briggs Martin, 156
Yuyi Morales, 160
Nancy Winslow Parker, 164
John Paterson and Katherine Paterson,
    168

Booklists (*Cont.*)
  Katherine Paterson, 168
  Jeni Reeves, 172
  Dian Curtis Regan, 176
  Barbara Santucci, 180
  April Pulley Sayre, 184
  Janet Stevens, 188
  Tanya Lee Stone, 192
  Anastasia Suen, 196
  Jane Yolen/Heidi Elisabet Yolen
    Stemple, 199–200
Booklists
  100 Days Tales, 128
  Anasazi, 10
  Apple Books, 100
  Baking Mishaps, 4
  Baseball Cards—More Stories and
    Information, 111
  Books about Rice, 40
  Books about Vegetables and Nutrition,
    188
  Bread of All Kinds, 172
  Cake Connections, 196
  Chocolate Books, 200
  Collaborative Books: Read and Compare
    with *One Dog Canoe*, 54
  Coming to America, 36
  Cookie Books, 72
  cranberries, 8
  Cucumbers to Pickles, 96
  Dirt and Compost—Gardening, 25
  Gingerbread Books, 16
  Great-Granny and Little Red Hen, 66
  History of the Statue of Liberty, 36
  Immigration, 152
  Learning More about Space, 84
  Monkeys and Bananas, 48
  More Books: Appalachian Settings, 124
  More Information about Marco Polo, 88
  More Pancake Books, 52
  More Tales from the Caribbean, 32
  Negro Baseball League, 107
  Never Enough Chocolate, 175
  Oranges in Books, 90
  Pasta*Pasta*Pasta, 86
  Pasta—From Field to Food, 184
  Pizza Books, 58

  Pumpkin Books, 44
  Read about Corn, 139
  Skeleton Books, 22
  Soups*Soups*Soups, 192
  Spinning the Gold (versions of the
    Rumpelstiltskin tale), 80
  Tortillas*Tortillas*Tortillas, 158
  Trading and Bartering, 156
  Water*Water*Water, 91
  World War II: The Dutch Experience
    and Others, 168
  Zucchini books, 180
Books about Rice (booklist), 40
Books about Vegetables and Nutrition
  (booklist), 188
Bread of All Kinds (booklist), 172
Bridge to Terabithia, The, 166
Broccoli, 59
Brownies, 176
Bryan, Ashley, xi, 29–32, 32 (booklist)
Bugs, 161
Bumblebee Stew—A Story, 147
Bunting, Eve, 33–36, 36 (booklist)
Butler, Dori Hillestad, 37–40, 40
  (booklist)
Buzzeo, Toni, 41–44, 44 (booklist)
Bynum, Janie, xi, 45–48, 49 (booklist)

Cake Connections (booklist), 196
Carle, Eric, xi, 49–52, 50 (booklist)
Casanova, Mary, 53–56, 56 (booklist)
Caseley, Judith, xi, 57–60, 60 (booklist)
Castro, Andres, 73
Catalyst, 5
Cecil, Ivon, 174
Celebrations, patriotic, 34
Chelsey and the Green-Haired Kid, 105,
  106
Chicken Soup by Heart, 113, 114
Chicks and Chickens, 98
Child's Calendar, A, 117
Chocolate Books (booklist), 200
Climo, Shirley, 61–64, 63 (booklist)
cocoa powder, 54
Collaborative Books: Read and Compare
  with *One Dog Canoe* (booklist), 54
Coming to America (booklist), 36

Confe$$ion$ and $ecrets of Howard J. Fingerhut, 114
coo-coo, 78
Cook-a-Doodle-Do, 65, 66
Cookie Books (booklist), 72
cookies, 69, 70
Corn, 137
Cornbread and Chess Pie, 170–71
cornbread, 122, 170
cou-cou, 78
couscous, 142
Cow Who Wouldn't Come Down, The, 121
Cranberries and Jell-O, 8
Cranberries, 8 (booklist)
Crummel, Susan Stevens, 65–68, 68 (booklist)
Cucumbers to Pickles (booklist), 96
Cummings, Pat, 69–72, 71–72 (booklist)

D Is for Dreidel: A Hanukkah Alphabet Book, 189
deLaboulaye, Eduoard, 35
Dem Bones, 22
Deuker, Carl, 73–76, 76 (booklist)
Dillon, Diane, 77–80, 79 (booklist)
Dillon, Leo, 77–80, 79 (booklist)
Dirt and Compost—Gardening (booklist), 25
Dork in Disguise, 106
Dyson, Marianne J., 81–84, 84 (booklist)
Family recipes, 14
Feeney, Kathy, xi, 85–88, 88 (booklist)
Finest Horse in Town, The, 153
Flame of Peace, The, 141
Fraiser, Debra, 89–92, 92 (booklist)
fungi, 78

Gaber, Susan, 93–6, 96 (booklist)
Gibbons, Gail, 97–100, 99–100 (booklist)
Gingerbread Books (booklist), 16
Gingerbread Man, The, 14
Girl Who Spun Gold, The, 77
Goble, Paul, xi, 101–4, 104 (booklist)
goditas, 157
Gorman, Carol, 105–8, 108 (booklist)
Great Gilly Hopkins, The, 166
Great Tooth Fairy Rip-Off, 37

Great-Granny and Little Red Hen (booklist), 66
Gutman, Dan, 109–12, 112 (booklist)

Hale, Sara Josepha, 7
Hamilton, Virginia, 77
Handful of Dirt, A, 26
Hanlon, Beverly, 174
Hanna's Hog, 13
Hershenhorn, Esther, 113–16, 116 (booklist)
Honey Makers, The, 98
Hot Marshmallow Cheesecake with Raspberry Fudge Sauce, xi
How I Became a Pirate, 148
Hunt, Roger Morris, 35
Hunter, Dia, 174
Hyman, Trina Schart, xi, 117–20, 120 (booklist)

I Wonder What's Under There?!—a Brief History of Underwear, 141
Iktomi and the Buffalo Berries, 101
Iktomi, 102
illustrative credits, 202–3
Immigration (booklist), 152
injera, 133
introduction, xi
inventions, 82–83
Island of the Skog, xi, 129

Johnson, Paul Brett, 121–24, 123 (booklist)
Just a Minute: A Trickster Tale and Counting Book, 157

Kasza, Keiko, 125–28, 127 (booklist)
Kellogg, Steven, xi, 129–32, 132 (booklist)
Kurtz, Jane, iii, xi, 133–36, 136 (booklist)

Lamp, The Ice, and the Boat Called Fish, *The,* 153
Land Ho! 50 Glorious Years in the Age of Exploration, 169
Landau, Elaine, 137–40, 140 (booklist)

Lanton, Sandy, xi
Lattimore, Deborah Nourse, 141–44, 144 (booklist)
Lazarus, Emma, 35
Learning More about Space (booklist), 84
lefse, 37, 39
Long, Melinda, 145–48, 145 (booklist)
Love from Aunt Betty, 162

M Is for Minnesota, 38
Mac & Cheese, 182
Maestro, Betsy, 149–52, 149 (booklist)
Magic and Mischief: Tales from Cornwall, 62
Marco Polo Bars, xi
Marco Polo: Explorer of China, 85
Marge's Diner, 98
Martin, Jacqueline Briggs, 153–56, 156 (booklist)
Martindale, Elaine (Ashley Bryan's Sister), xi, 29, 30
metate, 157
Midsummer Night's Dork, 106
Miss Birdie Chose a Shovel, 18
Monkeys and Bananas (booklist), 48
Moose Tracks, 53
Morales, Yuyi, 157–60, 160 (booklist)
More Books with a Connection to Coconut Cake (booklist), 155
More Books: Appalachian Settings (booklist), 124
More Information about Marco Polo (booklist), 88
More Pancake Books (booklist), 52
More Tales from the Caribbean (booklist), 32
Mother for Choco, A, 125
Mulligatawany, 114
My Lucky Day, 125

NASA, 82–83
Negro Baseball League (booklist), 107
Never Enough Chocolate (booklist), 175
Noodle Man: The Pasta Superhero, 181

On Sand Island, 153
On the Day You Were Born, 89

On the Town: A Community Adventure, 57
One Dog Canoe, 54
Oranges in Books (booklist), 90
oranges, 90
Origin of Rocco's Broccoli So That You Can Eat Ice Cream Later, 59

pancakes, 52
Parker, Nancy Winslow, xi, 161–64, 164 (booklist)
Pasta Facts, 182–83
Pasta*Pasta*Pasta (booklist), 86
Pasta—From Field to Food (booklist), 184
Pecan facts, 22
Pecan pie, 21
Persian Cinderella, 61
photograph credits, 201–2
Picnic in October, A, 33
Pineapple Upside-Down Cake Trivia, 194
pineapple upside-down cake, 194
Pizza Books (booklist), 58
pizza, 57
Plaidypus Lost, 67
Polo, Marco, 87
potato dumplings, 51
potatoes, sweet, 31
Potter, Beatrix, 13
Preparing for the Festival, 119
President's Cabinet and How It Grew, The, 161
Prince of the Golden Ox, The, 141
Prom, 5
Pulitzer, Joseph, 35
Pumpkin Blossoms, 42
Pumpkin Books (booklist), 44

Queen Wilhelmina in American, 167
Quick Corn Facts, 138
Quilting Bee, 98
quotations credits, 203–4

Read about Corn (booklist), 139
Reeves, Jeni, xi, 169–72, 172 (booklist)
Regan, Dian Curtis, 173–76, 176 (booklist)

Retsina wine, 142
rice, wild, 38
Roger, Jacqueline, 114
Ronneburg Restaurant, xi
Root, Phyllis, 93

Santorini (Island), 142
Santucci, Barbara, xi, 177–80, 180 (booklist)
Sayre, April Pulley, 181–84, 184 (booklist)
Sea Chest, 41
Seasons of Arnold's Apple Tree, The, 97
Serpent Slayer: and Other Stories of Strong Women, The, 117, 118
Seuss, Dr., 13
Shoetown, 65
Sisters, 57
Skeleton Books (booklist), 22
Sneetches, The, 13
Snowflake Bentley, 153
Soups*Soups*Soups (booklist), 192
Sour Cream—What Is It?, 151
sources for more information, 206
Speak, 5,
spinach quiche, 70
Spinning the Gold (versions of the Rumpelstiltskin tale) (booklist), 80
Statue of Liberty, 33, 34, 35, 36
Stemple, Heidi E. Y. *See* Stemple, Heidi Elisabet Yolen
Stemple, Heidi Elisabet Yolen, xi, 197–200, 199–200 (booklist)
Stevens, Janet, 185–88, 188 (booklist)
Stone, Charles P., 35
Stone, Tanya Lee, iii, xi, 189–92, 192 (booklist)
Stumptown Kid, 105, 106
Suen, Anastasia, 193–96, 196 (booklist)
sugar cookie, 14
sweet potatoes, 31

Tale of Peter Rabbit, The, 13
Tale of Tricky Fox, The, 14
Tchana, Katrin, 117–20, 120 (booklist)
Ten Sleepy Sheep, 93
Texas Writers' Potluck Menu, 174
Thanksgiving, 5
Thanksgiving dinner, 6
There Goes Lowell's Party, 114
To Market, To Market, 185
To test for soft ball stage, 147
tortillas, 157, 159
Tortillas*Tortillas*Tortillas (booklist), 158
Tortoise and the Hare, The, 185
Trading and Bartering (booklist), 156
Turkey Pox, 5
Turtle Knows Your Name, 29
Two Giants, The, 33

waffle cookies, 130
waffles, 130
wat, 133
Water*Water*Water (booklist), 91
watercolors, 132
Webster, Chery, 174
What Do These Books Have in Common? (Zucchini), 180
What Is Russian Borscht?, 150
White, E. B., ii
wild rice, 38
Willie McLean and the Civil War Surrender, 170–71
Willis, Pat, 174
Wolfe, Rosalyn, 174
Wolf's Chicken Stew, The, 125
Word or Two from Dan Gutman, A, 110
World War II: The Dutch Experience and Others (booklist), 168

Yolen, Jane, xi, 197–200, 199–200 (booklist)

Zucchini books (booklist), 180
Zucchini, 178–79, 180

Recipe Index

Altoona Baboona's Banana Nut Bread, 47
Ambrosia, 92
Ambrosia Cake—Oranges and Coconut, 91
Anasazi Bean Soup, 11
Anasazi Beans, 11
Anastasia's Mother's Chocolate Chip
    Cookies, 195
Appalachian Corn Bread, 122
Apricot Sherbet, 63
Arnold's Apple Pie, 99

Baklava, 94
Banana Bake, 46
Banana Nut Bread, Altoona Baboona's, 47
Banan-O Choc-O Pops and Nutty Spots, 47
Barley and Mushroom Kielbasa Soup, 190
Basic Quesadillas, 158
Beans, Anasazi, 11
berry syrup, 103
Birthday Cake Supreme, 3
Birthday Cake, Neapolitan, 35
Blueberry Muffins, 167
Blueberry Pound Cake, 166
Bread pudding, 30
bread, warm, 134
bread, zucchini, 179
broccoli, 59
Brownies, Curtis, 176
Buffalo Berry Preserves (and syrup), 103
Buffalo Berry Sweet and Sour Sauce, 103
Bumblebee Stew (Oyster Stew), 148
Bumbleberry Pie, 98

Cake, Ambrosia, 91
Cake, Birthday Cake Supreme, 3
Cake, Crazy Eggless Chocolate, 56
Cake, history of, 134
Cake, Mystery Writer's, 2
Cake, pineapple upside-down, 104
Cake, pound, 103
Cake, Royal Chocolate, 198

Cake, zucchini chocolate, 178
Caramelized Onion Marmalade, 162
Cheesecake, 131-32
Cherry Berry Parfait, 74
Chicken—Southern Pecan Baked, 25
Chicken Soup, homemade, 114
Chicken, Old Drye Frye, 123
Chicken, Saffron, 83
Chinese Rice Cakes, 119
Chocolate cake, 198
Chocolate Cherry Nut Cookies, Double
    Dutch, 55
Chocolate Chip Cookies (Wolf's), 126
chocolate chip cookies, Anastasia's
    Mother's, 195
Chocolate Chip, oatmeal cookies, 71
Chocolate Lover's No Bake Cookies, 175
Chocolate Mousse, 106
Chocolate Pecan Pie, 191
Chocolate Zucchini Cake, 178
Chocolate, Crazy Eggless cake, 56
Chopped Vegetable Salad B la Andres
    Castro, 76
Cinnamon Rolls, Mary Azarian's, 19
Coconut Cake, 155
Coconut Cream Pie (Monkey Pie), 64
Codfish Cakes, 78
Coffee cake, 134
Coffee cake, Sour Cream, 151
Cookie Eater's Oatmeal Chocolate Chip
    Cookies, 71
Cookies, 71
Cookies, chocolate chip, 195
Cookies, Double Dutch—Chocolate
    Cherry Nut, 55
Cookies, Gingerbread People, 14
Cookies, Minnie's Sherman's Sour
    Cream, 152
Cookies, no bake chocolate lover's, 175
Cookies, Sugar Cookies for Friends, 60
Cookies, Wolf's Chocolate Chip, 126

Corn Bread Casserole, 138
Corn Bread, Appalachian, 122
Corn Salad, 139
Cornbread, skillet, 170
Cornish Pasty, 62
Cowboy Coffee Cake, 134
Cranberry Jell-O, 8
Crazy Eggless Chocolate Cake, 56
Cucumbers, 95
Cupcakes, Surprise Celebration, 34
Curtis Brownies, 176
Dori's Grandmother's Lefse
    (Hardangerlefse), 39
Double Dutch—Chocolate Cherry Nut
    Cookies, 55
Dumplings, potato, 51

Fruit and Nut Salad, 111
Fudge, Norm's Chocolate Fudge Coconut
    Balls, 15
Fudge, Norm's Chocolate, 15
German Pancakes, 52
German Potato Salad, 27
Gingerbread People (cookies), 14
Granny Serafina's Chocolate Waffle
    Cookies, 130

Hardengerlefse, 39
History of Cake, 134
Homemade Chicken Soup, 114
Hot Chocolate, 199

Jade's Strawberry Shortcake, 66
jam, strawberry, 134
Jell-O, 8
Jenny's Hot Marshmallow Cheesecake with
    Raspberry Fudge Sauce, 131-32

latkes, 191
Latkes, Tanya's Grandmother's, 191
Lefse, 39

Mac & Cheese, 182
Mama's Chess Pie, 172
Marco Polo Bars, 87
MarcoRoni, 86
Marmalade, caramelized onions, 162

Mary Azarian's Cinnamon Rolls, 19
Mexican Roll-ups, 66
Minnie Sherman's Sour Cream Cookies,
    152
Monkey Pie aka Coconut Cream Pie, 64
Muffins, blueberry, 167
Mulligatawny, 114
My Mother's Potato Salad, 127
Mystery Writer's Cake, 2

Neapolitan Birthday Cake, 35
Norm's Chocolate Fudge Coconut Balls,
    15
Norm's Chocolate Fudge, 15

Oatmeal Chocolate Chip Cookies, Cookie
    Eater's, 71
Old Drye Frye Chicken, 123
Orange Julius, 110
Orange Spirals, 135
Oyster stew, 148

Pancakes, German, 52
Parfait, Cherry Berry, 74
Pasta, soup-er, 183
Pat Cumming's Spinach Surprise, 70
Peanut Butter Pie, 146
Pecan Pie, Southern, 25
Pickles, Raymond's Dill, 25
Pie Pastry, 98
Pie, Arnold's Apple, 99
Pie, Bumbleberry, 98
Pie, Chocolate Pecan, 191
Pie, Mama's Chess, 172
Pie, Peanut Butter, 146
Pie, Pumpkin Pizzazz, 42
Pie, Southern Pecan, 25
Pie, Sweet Potato, 31
Pineapple Sweet Yams, 82
Pineapple Upside-down Cake, 104
Pinenut Couscous, 142
Plaintain Fritters, 79
Potato Dumplings, 51
potato salad, 127
Potato Salad, German, 27
Potekaker, 39
Pound Cake, 103

pound cake, blueberry, 166
pudding, bread, 30
Pumpkin Blossoms, cooking, 42
Pumpkin Pie Pizzazz, 42
Pumpkin Pizzazz Roll, 7
Pumpkins, baking the, 42

Quesadillas, basic, 158

Raymond's Dill Pickles, 25
Rice Soup, Wild, 38
Rocco's Broccoli So That You Can Eat Ice
    Cream Later, 59
Rolls (orange spirals), 135
Royal Chocolate Cake, 198
Russian Borscht, 150

Saffron Chicken, 83
Salad, Vegetable Manifesto Lettuce, 186
Shrimp Santorini, 143
Signature Recipes
    Caroline Arnold, 11
    Jim Aylesworth, 15
    Mary Azarian, 19
    Bob Barner, 23
    Raymond Bial, 26, 27
    Ashley Bryan (Bryan's sister Elaine
    Martindale), 30, 31
    Dori Hillestad Butler, 38, 39
    Janie Bynum, 47
    Mary Casanova, 46
    Judith Caseley, 59
    Susan Crummel, 67
    Pat Cummings, 70
    Gail Gibbons, 99
    Keiko Kasza, 127
    Jane Kurtz, 133
    Deborah Nourse Lattimore, 143
    Melinda Long, 148
    Besty Maestro, 152
    Jacqueline Briggs Martin, 155
    Katherine Paterson, 168
    Jeni Reeves, 170, 171
    Dian Curtis Regan, 176

    April Pulley Sayre, 183
    Tanya Lee Stone, 191
    Suen, Anastasia, 195
Skillet Cornbread, 170
Soup, Anasazi Bean, 11
Soup, Barley and Mushroom Kielbasa, 190
Soup, Vegetable Potato Soup for Fifteen,
    187
Soup, Wild Rice, 38
Soup-er Pasta, 183
Sour Cream Coffee Cake, 151
Sour Cream Cookies, Minnie Sherman's,
    152
Southern Pecan Baked, Chicken, 25
Southern Pecan Pie, 25
Spaghetti on a Shoestring, 106
Spinach Surprise, 70
Stew, Oyster, 148
Strawberry Jam, 134
Strawberry shortcake, Jade's, 66
Sugar Cookies for Friends, 60
Surprise Celebration Cupcakes, 34
Sweet and Sour Sauce, 103
Sweet Potato Pie, 31

Tom's Potato Lefse (Potekaker), 39
Tortillas, 159

Vegetable Manifesto Lettuce Salad, 186
Vegetable Potato Soup for Fifteen, 187
Vegetable Salad, 76
Vinegar Cucumbers and Onions, 95

Waffle Cookies, 130
Warm Bread, 134
Wild Rice Soup, 38
Wolf's Chocolate Chip Cookies, 126

Yams, Pineapple Sweet, 82
Yogurt and Mustard Seed Cucumbers, 95

Zucchini Bread, 179
Zucchini, Sautéed with Lemon, 178

About the Authors

SHARRON L. MCELMEEL is the founder of McBookwords—a literacy organization and an instructor at the University of Wisconsin—Stout, Menomonie, Wisconsin where she teaches courses in children's literature and young adult literature. She is also a writer and educational consultant who has built a national reputation in the area of children's and young adult literature is an often-requested conference speaker. She was named Iowa Reading Teacher of the Year in 1987, and in 2003 she received the Iowa Reading Association's State Literacy Award in recognition of her lifelong efforts to build literacy and literature appreciation in the community. In 2004, she was named one of the top ten online educators by Innovative Teaching newsletter. She maintains a Web site at http://www.mcelmeel.com.

DEBORAH L. MCELMEEL earned a graduate degree in science from the University of Iowa and after teaching for several years in the Chicago Public School system she now teaches chemistry at Stoughton High School, Stoughton, Wisconsin. Her background includes experience in a family restaurant, the University of Iowa kitchens, managing a catering business, and culinary positions in several specialty restaurants. Gourmet cooking and recipe development has been a life-long avocation.